Contents

BELLS AND TRACKS (1966)

SEEING IN THE DARK (1970)

THE WILD MARKET-SQUARE (1983)

RECENT POEMS

Introduction

Tomas Tranströmer was born in Stockholm in 1931. Between 1954 and 1983 he published nine collections of poems whose qualities are such that for the past thirty years he has been one of the most highly regarded figures in contemporary Swedish poetry. He is also one of the most-translated of living Swedish poets and his reading tours take him all over the world. As well as shorter selections published in over twenty languages, larger selections have appeared in Spanish, Dutch, Hungarian, German, and of course English. American poets who have translated his work include Robert Bly, Samuel Charters and May Swenson. There is a large and growing body of critical articles and interviews scattered in many periodicals and newspapers, and in 1983 his fellow-poet Kjell Espmark brought out a substantial study of his poetry (*Resans formler/The Journey's Formulae*, Norstedts, Stockholm).

For most of his adult life he has worked as a psychologist, but this preference for an "ordinary" or "non-literary" way of earning his living should not be seen as implying any kind of division of his life into separate areas. In an interview with Gunnar Harding in 1973 he replied as follows to the question of how his writing relates to his work as a psychologist:

> I believe there is a very close connection, though it can't be seen. Everything one writes is an expression of a gathered experience. And the problems one meets in the world at large are present to a very great extent in what I write, though it doesn't always show directly. But it's close to hand, all the time. That's what makes me feel under such a pressure when I write. What I put down on paper must be able to exist together with that, the total and rather dark picture of the world. And that's true even when I'm writing about something which doesn't seem to touch that total picture.

Tranströmer is perhaps less in need of selection or pruning than many other poets, but even so the new reader will probably not want to plod through this volume straight from A to Z. Reading back from recent to early work could be more helpful than reading forward chronologically – an approach invited by the arrangement of May Swenson's selection (*Windows and Stones*, University of Pittsburgh Press, 1972). Whichever direction the new reader wants to follow, a few pointers may help.

17 Poems (1954) gathered pieces written by Tranströmer in his late teens and very early twenties and immediately announced the presence of a distinct poetic personality. The three longer pieces which conclude the collection suggest a kind of poetic ambition which the young Tranströmer soon lost – his notes on my first version of 'Elegy' for instance contain remarks like 'This poem was written by a romantic 22-year-old!' and 'Oh dear, how complicated I was in my younger days . . .' But the

very first poem, suitably called 'Prelude', reveals a quality characteristic
of all his writing, and that is the very sharply realised visual sense of
his poems. The images leap out from the page, so the first-time reader
or listener has the feeling of being given something very tangible, at
once. In a way this quality seems to facilitate the translation – or rather
the exportation – of these poems, at least to the extent that sharply
defined images may be "transposed" into another language. Poets like
Pär Lagerkvist or Harry Martinson, much of whose work depends on
very specific resonances of the Swedish language, are liable to lose
much more in translation, and may indeed resist the process almost
completely. Labouring over vowels and consonants may never have had
much attraction for Tranströmer, but I think it is worth stressing for
the foreign reader that in Tranströmer we are not dealing with any kind
of "minimal" East European poet: he is very particular about the rhythm
of his lines (sometimes the translator can find a parallel, sometimes he
can't) and in the original Swedish his poems have an individual and
unmistakable music of their own (I doubt if the translator can talk about
"parallels" in any meaningful sense here).

'Prelude' also points forward thematically. It describes the process
of waking up (note how this process appears not in the usual terms of
rising to the surface but in terms of falling, of a parachute jump down
into a vivid and teeming world). And this fascination with the borders
between sleep and waking, with the strange areas of access between an
everyday world we seem to know and another world we can't know in
the same way but whose presence is undeniable – such a fascination
has over the decades been one of Tranströmer's predominant themes.
A recent poem, 'Dream Seminar', from *The Wild Market-Square* (1983)
deals directly with certain aspects of the relations between waking and
dreaming states, but the reader will soon discover many poems which
explore this region.

The way in which much or even most of Tranströmer's poetry
describes, or allows for, or tries to come to terms with the powerful
elements of our lives which we cannot consciously control or even satis-
factorily define suggests, rightly, that there is a profoundly religious
aspect to his response to the world and therefore in his poetry. In a
largely secular country like Sweden such a writer may well be asked
about religion in rather a blunt or naive manner (as if 'Do you believe
in God?' were the same kind of question as 'Do you vote Social Demo-
crat?') and Tranströmer has always replied to such questions cautiously.
The following (from the Gunnar Harding interview already mentioned)
is a characteristic response to the comment that reviewers sometimes
refer to him as a mystic and sometimes as a religious poet:

Very pretentious words, mystic and so on. Naturally I feel reserved about their use, but you could at least say that I respond to reality in such a way that I look on existence as a great mystery and that at times, at certain moments, this mystery carries a strong charge, so that it does have a religious character, and it is often in such a context that I write. So these poems are all the time pointing towards a greater context, one that is incomprehensible to our normal everyday reason. Although it begins in something very concrete.

This movement towards a larger context is very important and it reflects Tranströmer's distrust of over-simple formulations, slogans and rhetorical gestures as short-cuts that can obscure and mislead. It is in similar terms that we can see his response (or perhaps refusal to respond directly) to the criticism of several reviewers of the late 1960s and early 1970s that his poetry ignored current political "realities". The assumption behind such criticism was that poetry is just another element of political debate and its use of language is no different from the leader-writer's use of language. Many of his poems do deal with current "realities", but with a careful avoidance of the simplifications and aggressions of politicised language and with an awareness of a wider and deeper context that seemed beyond the range of the directly "engaged" poetry of the period, with its concern for taking "positions" on a black-and-white and rather parochial political map. See in particular 'About History' from Bells and Tracks (1966), and then 'By the River', 'Outskirts', 'Traffic' and 'Night Duty' from Seeing in the Dark (1970).

To return to the religious aspects – the reader will notice how specifically or overtly religious allusions in the early poetry soon disappear from succeeding work. This has been interpreted as a process of secularisation: I would rather see it as a way of trying to do without the short-hand of everyday religious terminology in order to try to define for oneself those areas in which a sense of immanence may be experienced. We see something of this attempt in poems like 'Secrets on the Way' and 'Tracks', both in Tranströmer's 1958 collection, where a series of contrasts, or similes, or just luminously clear images, are grouped as if round a central space where some kind of epiphany is or may be or has been experienced. Such poems end by returning us, perhaps abruptly, to an active world, but they leave us with the feeling that a strangeness has crossed our path.

Later forms of this development seem to entail two processes. First, we can see some attempt to be more specific about this central space or crossing-point, about this "something" which by intruding can illuminate or disturb our "normal" way of life: here we can find paradoxes, imagery from and about dreams, speculations about how both past and future can impinge upon the present, investigations into memory, and a fascination with the many ways in which borders, open and closed, may be experienced. Second, we find a gradual move away from the impersonality of the early poetry. Tranströmer can still use the third person singular as a means of giving distance to what is clearly first-person singular experience – but from the late 1960s and the early 1970s we can watch an increasingly open involvement of the poet's own personality as an element in the poems. This is partly a matter of allowing more of the concrete starting-point of the poem to appear in the poem (Tranströmer can name a birth-place for nearly every poem), but it is also, more importantly, a matter of letting himself appear in his poems as, in a sense, an actor in his own dramas, both acting and being acted upon or through. This process can be clearly followed in poems such as: 'Lament', in *The Half-Finished Heaven* (1962); 'Crests', 'Winter's Formulae' and 'Alone', in *Bells and Tracks* (1966); 'Preludes', 'Upright' and 'The Bookcase' in *Seeing in the Dark* (1970); 'The Outpost' and 'December 1972' in *Paths* (1973).

    The lines of development I have roughly indicated reach a peak – or perhaps a wave-crest may be more appropriate, for it is something in motion – in *Baltics* (1974), Tranströmer's longest poem to date and one which marked a new expansiveness in his manner. Note the plural of the title: here we have not one Baltic but a whole series of them, reflecting the very different experience of those in whose lives that particular sea has come to play a part; some of these Baltics overlap, while some apparently contradict each other. The poem seems to have been under way by about 1970 and two external stimuli helped as starting-points. One was the finding of a log-book kept by his (maternal) grandfather in the 1880s, listing the ships he piloted (this is quoted from in Part One). The other was his reading of Edward Lucie-Smith's English translation of part of Jean Paul de Dadelsen's *Jonah*, which suggested to him a manner or tone of voice for a long poem less monumental than the accents of Eliot in *Four Quartets*. A third element should be mentioned and that is Tranströmer's life-long interest in poems whose growth parallels musical development: to give only two examples, the three long pieces which conclude *17 Poems* (and which were originally meant to constitute one long poem) were intended to represent a parallel to passacaglia form, and 'The Four Temperaments' in *Secrets on the Way* aimed to echo Hindemith's *Theme and Variations: 'The Four Temperaments'* for piano and string orchestra (1940). However much musical experience has undoubtedly inspired the poet, readers of the written text must decide for themselves in what sense *Baltics* fulfils Tranströmer's own claim that it is his 'most consistent attempt to write music'. At the very least, the pattern of thematic return and variation may recall similar patterns in many musical works. Tranströmer has further remarked that *Baltics* is in part a polemic against his earlier self, against the way in which his earlier poems from the Stockholm archipelago (the island of Runmarö has close family connections) treated the area as a protected oasis or reserve, whereas now *Baltics* treats the landscape and its life as open to the threats of the surrounding world.

The more relaxed manner of *Baltics* does not imply a more casual structure, however. It is not difficult for the reader new to the work to notice the arch-like patterning of themes, as outlined by the Danish critic Steen Andersen:

> Part Six, about the grandmother . . . is a parallel to Part One, about the grandfather; in both cases there is documentary knowledge about the family (photo, log-book) and in both cases the poet himself must enquire his way forward as regards other details of this past. From Part One, the sea, we are taken, in Part Two, to the land, but with many references to the life which Part One introduced and described to us; the churchyard stones seen by the I-figure unite past and present. In Part Three the I-figure is more present still, but here too mainly through observations of things left by the past (the font, a photo). Parts Four and Five describe immediate observations, as distinct from the family and historical memories we otherwise find in the book. And finally Part Six carries us back to the past (the grandmother) and to the present, especially in the closing lines . . . It is thus a matter of *people* in a particular *place*.

In its amplification of this outline, Kjell Espmark's account of *Baltics* lets us see the sequence as a climax in Tranströmer's work up to the early 1970s, and Espmark argues, rightly, that it is to its themes we must look to get to the heart of the poem. On the one hand we have distances, obstacles or frontiers; on the other we have attempts to overcome these, and even instances of spontaneous contact –

> The distance or blockage can change from one section to another – from historical and geographical distance to emotional isolation and the inability to articulate what 'wants to be said'. The bridging-over theme is modulated accordingly. The tension between the limiting and the uniting movements condenses in one point – a genuinely Tranströmerian oxymoron – 'the open frontier'. It is towards this epiphanously charged point that the movements of the poem strive.

In order to illustrate some of the foregoing, and also to give some idea of Tranströmer's own approach to his poems, it may be interesting to give a few examples from Tranströmer's own comments on his poems. He talks quite freely about his work and seems prepared to give his readers a great deal of freedom as to what they may find in his poems. Generally he is careful to avoid telling us what we ought to find:

The Journey's Formulae, first stanza (*Secrets on the Way*) (p.49)

I feel as untalented as a schoolboy suddenly left alone in a room with a beautiful lady and quite at a loss how to begin. Or like a detective at the start of an inquiry. Here is a man ploughing. It means something. Why have I now for half a year seen that man who is ploughing? No, it'll soon be a whole year. What does it mean? A month ago I finally understood what would happen. It's in Yugoslavia. At first I thought it was in a Swedish landscape in autumn – I was tricked by the lighting. No, it's Yugoslavia, in the middle of the day, and the sun is burning. It has something to do with the war. Or at least there are many dead people in the background – they move away later but what is really going on? It's no epic, it's a bagatelle, five lines perhaps. Yet terribly important to me . . .

[Letter to Göran Palm, 1956]

In the Nile Delta (*The Half-Finished Heaven*) (p.62)

In the first place it is a direct description of something I actually experienced. It is not something I invented – I recount in the concentrated form of the poem the experiences of a day in the town of Tanta in Egypt in 1959. I and my wife (who was only nineteen then and had never before been confronted with the reality of a poor country) had with difficulty managed to escape from the tour guides – there was never any help available if it was a matter of making one's way into parts of the country which the authorities did not want to show to foreigners – and there we were in Tanta. It could be asked why I use 'he' instead of 'I' in the poem – I think it is a way of giving distance and generality to a difficult and troubling experience. I have tried to write as unsentimentally and nakedly as possible and mainly with monosyllabic words. Well – we went to sleep in the indescribably dirty ex-hotel and then I dreamt what is in the poem. The words which a 'voice' said were somewhat different – as often happens in dreams the words were nonsense-words, but they had the meaning I've given them in the poem. The dream helped me, it created a change of mood from negative feelings and hate towards something else – not to a "reconciliation" with the suffering around us but it gave a chance of seeing it without running away. If I were to philosophise about this I would say that I believe hate and rage are a first and natural reaction to the plight of poor countries but they don't give much inspiration to do anything about it. In the dream there was a strongly positive element, a sort of GOOD WILL. My immediate reaction to this experience was of a religious nature and a trace of this can be seen in for instance the third to last line, in the words alluding to the Gospel account of the sick people around the pool in Bethesda – it was when the water stirred that the pool had its miracle-working power. [John 5.2] Many who are inimicable to religion kick blindly at things like this and think religion is a form of escapism, an attempt to conjure suffering away with some kind of false acceptance. But I hope that among the youngest generation of Christians, who are so active in the fight against poverty in the world, can show that their religious inspiration, on the contrary, gives them a chance of facing the problems directly and wanting to do something about them.

[In reply to a question from Mats Dahlberg, 1968]

Night Duty (*Seeing in the Dark*) (p.92)

That bell-ringing at the end of 'Night Duty' – when I was walking around in the old Västerås churchyard, which was in the process of being dug up, and caught sight of that digging-machine's scoop, bell-ringing broke out from the Lutheran cathedral tower and it seemed to wrap the whole experience in something which each reader can interpret as he pleases, but which for me is in part something fatefully apocalyptic but also something like the sponge of religious faith which is reached down from above to swab one's face as one sits like a beaten boxer in the corner of the ring waiting for the next round (the last one?).

[Letter to Göran Palm, 1970]

The Outpost (*Paths*) (p.100)

It began almost as a joke. It began very modestly. There was no intention it should become such a serious business, it was more something I passed the time with. The situation is this: I'm on a military exercise and get posted out to a heap of stones, a situation one experiences as quite absurd. And to cheer myself up a little I wrote the opening lines. I didn't mean any poem to come out of it. These first verses were written very easily just because I didn't have any feeling of 'now this is serious, you must achieve something'. But then gradually the poem came to deal with how I find myself in an absurd situation in life generally, as I often do. Life puts us in certain absurd situations and it's impossible to escape. And that's where the poem becomes very serious, in the fifth verse, which ends: 'I am the place / where creation is working itself out.' And that's a kind of religious idea which recurs here and there in my poems of late, that I see a kind of meaning in being present, in using reality, in experiencing it, in making something of it. And I have an inkling that I'm doing this as some sort of task or commission. It recurs further on in the book at the beginning of 'December Evening 1972' –

Here I come, the invisible man, perhaps employed
by a Great Memory to live right now . . .

It's a purely personal experience really, that I fulfil some function here,

in the service of something else. This sounds pretentious and because of that the tone in such circumstances often becomes a little frivolous.
[Conversation with Gunnar Harding, 1973]

Citoyens (*The Truth-Barrier*) (p.117)

It was in 1970, and I had an old Saab which had just been tested for roadworthiness. The verdict was that everything was in splendid order, including the brakes. Then when I was on the motorway, I found myself in a lane where everyone was driving fairly fast. Suddenly the cars in front of me slowed down. I stepped on the brakes but nothing happened. I drove right into the back of a Mercedes. My poor little car was like an accordeon. I survived. I stepped out. All I had was a shirt, a pair of trousers, shoes and a book about the French Revolution. That was all that was left after the accident. It was quite a shaking experience. I had a dream that night, and that is what I have recounted in the poem: I have not invented anything. Except perhaps the image of 'the plummet / that makes the clocks go . . .'
[Conversation with Robert Bly, 1977]

The Gallery (*The Truth-Barrier*) (p.123)

'The Gallery' is the poem I've had on the go longest – it began some time ten years ago. It started with a particular experience. I had been out as a teacher on a course for social workers, in interview techniques. It was in Laxå. In the evening I go to the motel to sleep and then I have a sort of Judgement Day experience: what is it I'm really doing? I'm a psychologist, after all, so I ought to be an expert in interviewing people. Playing one's professional role comes easily, and in that role one is to a high degree protected. But now I seemed to be confronted with what it really was about. It was a very disturbing evening. I lay there and seemed to see how the pictures of a whole crowd of people I had met in my job unwound like a film, and suddenly I seemed to experience them as a human being, not just as a professional. The poem is quite simply a coming-to-terms with this professional role, even if I started writing it as a rhapsody on authentic life-stories. Yes, all those fates glimpsed in the poem are authentic, and I myself am there too, in the passage beginning 'An artist said . . .' There you find a self-portrait, which was actually written in quite another context but which I inserted here. I thought that I too belonged in the gallery.
[Conversation with Matts Rying, 1979]

17 POEMS
17 DIKTER
(1954)

Prelude

Waking up is a parachute jump from dreams.
Free of the suffocating turbulence the traveller
sinks towards the green zone of morning.
Things flare up. From the viewpoint of the quivering lark
he is aware of the huge root-systems of the trees,
their swaying underground lamps. But above ground
there's greenery – a tropical flood of it – with
lifted arms, listening
to the beat of an invisible pump. And he
sinks towards summer, is lowered
in its dazzling crater, down
through shafts of green damp ages
trembling under the sun's turbine. Then it's checked,
this straight-down journey through the moment, and the wings spread
to the osprey's repose above rushing waters.
The bronze-age trumpet's
outlawed note
hovers above the bottomless depths.

In day's first hours consciousness can grasp the world
as the hand grips a sun-warmed stone.
The traveller is standing under the tree. After
the crash through death's turbulence, shall
a great light unfold above his head?

Autumnal Archipelago

Storm

Here the walker suddenly meets the giant
oak tree, like a petrified elk whose crown is
furlongs wide before the September ocean's
                    murky green fortress.

Northern storm. The season when rowanberry
clusters swell. Awake in the darkness, listen:
constellations stamping inside their stalls, high
                  over the tree-tops.

Evening – Morning

Moon – its mast is rotten, its sail is shrivelled.
Seagull – drunk and soaring away on currents.
Jetty – charred rectangular mass. The thickets
                  founder in darkness.

Out on doorstep. Morning is breaking, breaks in
ocean's greystone alleys and sun is sparkling
close to earth. Half-smothered, the gods of summer
                  fumble in sea-mist.

Ostinato

Under the buzzard's circling point of stillness
ocean rolls resoundingly on in daylight,
blindly chews its bridle of weed and snorts up
                  foam over beaches.

Earth is veiled in darkness where bats can sense their
way. The buzzard stops and becomes a star now.
Ocean rolls resoundingly on and snorts up
                  foam over beaches.

Five Stanzas to Thoreau

Yet one more abandoned the heavy city's
ring of greedy stones. And the water, salt and
crystal, closes over the heads of all who
                  truly seek refuge.

Silence slowly spiralling up has risen
here from earth's recesses to put down roots and
grow and with its burgeoning crown to shade his
                    sun-heated doorstep.

                    *

Kicks a mushroom thoughtlessly. Thunder clouds are
piling on the skyline. Like copper trumpets
crooked roots of trees are resounding, foliage
                    scatters in terror.

Autumn's headlong flight is his weightless mantle,
flapping till again from the frost and ashes
peaceful days have come in their flocks and bathe their
                    claws in the well-spring.

                    *

Disbelief will meet him who saw a geyser
and escaped from wells filled with stones, like Thoreau
disappearing deep in his inner greenness
                    artful and hopeful.

Gogol

The jacket threadbare as a wolf-pack.
The face like a marble slab.
Sitting in the circle of his letters in the grove that rustles
with scorn and error,
the heart blowing like a scrap of paper through the inhospitable
passageways.

The sunset is now creeping like a fox over this country,
igniting the grass in a mere moment.
Space is full of horns and hooves and underneath
the barouche glides like a shadow among my father's
lit courtyards.

St Petersburg on the same latitude as annihilation
(did you see the beauty in the leaning tower)
and round the ice-bound tenements floating like a jellyfish
the poor man in his cloak.

And here, enveloped in fasts, is the man who before was surrounded by
        the herds of laughter,
but these have long since taken themselves to tracts far above the tree-line.
Men's unsteady tables.
Look outside, see how darkness burns hard a whole galaxy of souls.
Rise up then on your chariot of fire and leave the country!

Sailor's Yarn

There are bare winter days when the sea is kin
to mountain country, crouching in grey plumage,
a brief minute blue, long hours with waves like pale
lynxes vainly seeking hold in the beach-gravel.

On such a day wrecks might come from the sea searching
for their owners, settling in the town's din, and drowned
crews blow landward, thinner than pipe-smoke.

(The real lynxes are in the north, with sharpened claws
and dreaming eyes. In the north, where day
lives in a mine both day and night.

Where the sole survivor may sit
at the borealis stove and listen
to the music of those frozen to death.)

Strophe and Counter-Strophe

The outermost circle belongs to myth. There the helmsman sinks upright
among glittering fish-backs.
How far from us! When day
stands in a sultry windless unrest –
as the Congo's green shadow holds
the blue men in its vapour –
when all this driftwood on the heart's sluggish
coiling current
piles up.

Sudden change: in under the repose of the constellations
the tethered ones glide.
Stern high, in a hopeless
position, the hull of a dream, black
against the coastline's pink. Abandoned
the year's plunge, quick
and soundless – as the sledge-shadow, dog-like, big
travels over snow,
reaches the wood.

Agitated Meditation

A storm drives the mill sails wildly round
in the night's darkness, grinding nothing. – You
    are kept awake by the same laws.
The grey shark belly is your weak lamp.

Shapeless memories sink to the sea's depths
and harden there to strange columns. – Green
    with algae is your crutch. A man
who takes to the seas comes back stiffened.

The Stones

The stones we threw I hear
fall, glass-clear through the years. In the valley
the confused actions of the moment
fly screeching from
treetop to treetop, become silent
in thinner air than the present's, glide
like swallows from hilltop
to hilltop until they've
reached the furthest plateaux
along the frontier of being. There all
our deeds fall
glass-clear
with nowhere to fall to
except ourselves.

Context

Look at the grey tree. The sky has run
through its fibres down in the earth –
only a shrunk cloud is left when
the earth has drunk. Stolen space
is twisted in pleats, twined
to greenery. – The brief moments
of freedom rise in us, whirl
through the Parcae and further.

Morning Approach

The black-backed gull, the sun-captain, holds his course.
Beneath him is the water.
The world is still sleeping like a
multicoloured stone in the water.
Undeciphered day. Days –
like aztec hieroglyphs.

The music. And I stand trapped
in its Gobelin weave with
raised arms – like a figure
out of folk art.

There is Peace in the Surging Prow

On a winter morning you feel how this earth
plunges ahead. Against the house walls
an air-current smacks
out of hiding.

Surrounded by movement: the tent of calm.
And the secret helm in the migrating flock.
Out of the winter gloom
a tremolo rises

from hidden instruments. It is like standing
under summer's high lime tree with the din
of ten thousand
insect wings above your head.

Midnight Turning Point

The wood-ant watches silently, looks into
nothing. And nothing's heard but drips from dim
leafage and the night's murmuring deep in
    summer's canyon.

The spruce stands like the hand of a clock,
spiked. The ant glows in the hill's shadow.
Bird cry! And at last. The cloud-packs slowly
    begin to roll.

Song

The gathering of white birds grew: gulls
dressed in canvas from the sails of foundered ships
but stained by vapours from forbidden shores.

Alarm! Alarm! round refuse from a cargo boat.
They crowded in and formed an ensign-staff
that signalled 'Booty here'.

And gulls careered across watery wastes
with blue acres gliding in the foam.
Athwart, a phosphorescent pathway to the sun.

But Väinämöinen travels in his past
on oceans glittering in ancient light.
He rides. The horse's hooves are never wet.

Behind: the forest of his songs is green.
The oak whose leap's a thousand years long.
The mighty windmill turned by birdsong.

And every tree a prisoner in its soughing.
With giant cones glinting in the moonlight
when the distant pine glows like a beacon.

Then the Other rises with his spell
and the arrow, seeing far and wide, flees,
the feather singing like a flight of birds.

A dead second when the horse abruptly
stiffens, breaks across the waterline
like a blue cloud beneath the thunder's touch.

And Väinämöinen plunges heavy in the sea
(a jumping-sheet the compass-points hold tight).
Alarm! Alarm! among the gulls around his fall!

Like one bewitched, without anxiety,
standing at the centre of the picture
of his joy, eleven corn-sheaves bulging.

Reliance – an alp-top humming in the ether
three thousand metres up where the clouds sail
races. The puffed basking shark wallows

guffawing soundlessly beneath the sea.
(Death and renewal when the wave arrives.)
And peacefully the breezes cycle through the leaves.

On the horizon thunder rumbles dully
(as the herd of buffalo flees in its dust).
The shadow of a fist clenches in the tree

and strikes down him who stands bewitched
in his joyous picture where the evening sky
seems to glow behind the wild-boar's mask of clouds.

His double, envious, arranges
a secret rendezvous with his woman.
And the shadow gathers and becomes a tidal wave

a tidal wave with riding seagulls darkened.
And the port-side heart sizzles in a breaker.
Death and renewal when the wave arrives.

The gathering of white birds grew: gulls
dressed in canvas from the sails of foundered ships
but stained by vapours from forbidden shores.

The herring-gull: a harpoon with a velvet back.
In close-up like a snowed-in hull
with hidden pulses glittering in rhythm.

His flier's nerves in balance. He soars.
Footless hanging in the wind he dreams
his hunter's dream with his beak's sharp shot.

He plunges to the surface, full-blossomed greed,
crams and jerks himself around his booty
as if he were a stocking. And then he rises like a spirit.

(Energies – their context is renewal,
more enigmatic than the eel's migrations.
A tree, invisible, in bloom. And as

the grey seal in its underwater sleep
rises to the surface, takes a breath
and dives – still asleep – to the seabed

so now the Sleeper in me secretly
has joined with *that* and has returned while I
stood staring fixedly at something else.)

And the diesel engine's throbbing in the flock
past the dark skerry, a cleft of birds
where hunger blossomed with stretched maw.

At night-fall they could still be heard:
an abortive music like that from
the orchestra pit before the play begins.

But on his ancient sea Väinämöinen drifted
shaken in the squall's mitt or supine
in the mirror-world of calms where the birds

were magnified. And from a stray seed, far
from land at the sea's edge growing
out of waves, out of a fogbank it sprang:

a mighty tree with scaly trunk, and leaves
quite transparent and behind them
the filled white sails of distant suns

glided on in trance. And now the eagle rises.

Elegy

At the outset. Like a fallen dragon
in some mist and vapour shrouded swamp,
our spruce-clad coastland lies. Far out there:
two steamers crying from a dream

in the fog. This is the lower world.
Motionless woods, motionless surface
and the orchid's hand that reaches from the soil.
On the other side, beyond these straits

but hanging in the same reflection: the Ship,
like the cloud hanging weightless in its space.
And the water round its prow is motionless,
becalmed. And yet – a storm is up!

and the steamer smoke blows level – the sun
flickers there in its grip – and the gale
is hard against the face of him who boards.
To make one's way up the port side of Death.

A sudden draught, the curtain flutters.
Silence ringing, an alarm clock.
A sudden draught, the curtain flutters.
Until a distant door is heard closing

far off in another year.

*

O field as grey as the buried bog-man's cloak.
And island floating darkly in the fog.
It's quiet, as when the radar turns
and turns its arc in hopelessness.

There's a crossroads in a moment.
Music of the distances converges.
All grown together in a leafy tree.
Vanished cities glitter in its branches.

From everywhere and nowhere a song
like crickets in the August dark. Embedded
like a wood-beetle, he sleeps here in the night,
the peat-bog's murdered traveller. The sap compels

his thoughts up to the stars. And deep
in the mountain: here's the cave of bats.
Here hang the years, the deeds, densely.
Here they sleep with folded wings.

One day they'll flutter out. A throng!
(From a distance, smoke from the cave mouth.)
But still their summer-winter sleep prevails.
A murmuring of distant waters. In the dark tree

a leaf that turns.

*

One summer morning a harrow catches
in dead bones and rags of clothing. – He
lay there after the peat-bog was drained
and now stands up and goes his way in light.

In every parish eddies golden seed
round ancient guilt. The armoured skull
in the ploughed field. A wanderer en route
and the mountain keeps an eye on him.

In every parish the marksman's tube is humming
at midnight when the wings unfold
and the past expands in its collapse
and darker than the heart's meteorite.

An absence of spirit makes the writing greedy.
A flag begins to smack. The wings
unfold around the booty. This proud journey!
where the albatross ages to a cloud

in Time's jaws. And culture is a whaling-
station where the stranger walks
among white gables, playing children, and
still with each breath he takes he feels

the murdered giant's presence.

                    *

Soft black-cock crooning from the heavenly spheres.
The music, guiltless in our shadow, like
the fountain water rising among the wild beasts,
deftly petrified around the playing jets.

The bows disguised, a forest.
The bows like rigging in a torrent –
the cabin's smashed beneath the torrent's hooves –
within us, balanced like a gyroscope, is joy.

This evening the world's calm is reflected
when the bows rest on strings without being moved.
Motionless in mist the forest trees
and the water-tundra mirroring itself.

Music's voiceless half is here, like the scent
of resin round lightning-damaged spruce.
An underground summer for each of us.
There at the crossroads a shadow breaks free

and runs off to where the Bach trumpet points.
Sudden confidence, by grace. To leave behind
one's self-disguise here on this shore
where the wave breaks and slides away, breaks

and slides away.

Epilogue

December. Sweden is a beached
unrigged ship. Against the twilight sky
its masts are sharp. And twilight lasts
longer than day – the road here is stony:
not till midday does the light arrive
and winter's colosseum rise
lit by unreal clouds. At once
the white smoke rises, coiling from
the villages. The clouds are high on high.
The sea snuffles at the tree-of-heaven's roots
distracted, as if listening to something else.
(Over the dark side of the soul
there flies a bird, wakening
the sleepers with its cries. The refractor
turns, catches in another time,
and it is summer: mountains bellow, bulged
with light and the stream raises the sun's glitter
in transparent hand . . . All then gone
as when a film spills out of a projector.)

Now the evening star burns through the cloud.
Houses, trees and fences are enlarged, grow
in the soundless avalanche of darkness.
And beneath the star there comes to light more
of the other, hidden landscape, that which lives
the life of contours on the night's X-ray.
A shadow pulls its sledge between the houses.
They are waiting.
                    Six o'clock – the wind
leaps out with noise along the village street,

in darkness, like a troop of horsemen. How
the black turmoil resounds and echoes!
The houses trapped in a dance of immobility,
the din like that of dreams. Gust upon gust
staggers over the bay away
to the open sea that tosses in the dark.
In space the stars are signalling despair.
They're lit and quenched by headlong clouds
that only when they shade the light betray
their presence, like clouds from the past that go
hunting in the souls. When I walk past
the stable wall I hear in all that noise
the sick horse tramping inside.
And there's departure in the storm,
by a broken gate that bangs and bangs, a lamp
swaying from a hand, a beast that cackles
frightened on the hill. Departure in the thunderous
rumble over the byre roofs, the roaring
in the telephone wires, the shrill whistling
in the tiles on night's roof
and the tree tossing helplessly.

A wail of bagpipes is let loose! A wail
of bagpipes keeping step! Liberators.
A procession. A forest on the march!
A bow-wave seethes and darkness stirs,
and land and water move. And the dead,
gone under deck, they are with us,
with us on the way: a voyage, a journey
which is no wild rush but gives security.
And the world is always taking down its tent
anew. One summer day the wind takes hold
of the oak's rigging, hurls Earth forward.
The lily paddles with its hidden webbed foot
in the pond's embrace – the pond which is in flight.
A boulder rolls away in the halls of space.
In the summer twilight islands seem to rise
on the horizon. Old villages are on
their way, retreating further into woods
on the seasons' wheels with magpie-creaking.
When the year kicks off its boots, and the sun
climbs higher, the trees break out in leaves
and take the wind and sail out in freedom.

Below the mountain stands the pinewood slope,
but summer's long warm breaker comes,
flows through the treetops slowly, rests
a moment, sinks away again –
a leafless coast remains. And finally:
God's spirit, like the Nile: flooding
and sinking in a rhythm calculated
in texts from many epochs.

But He is also the immutable
and thus observed here seldom. It's from
the side He crosses the procession's path.

As when the steamer passes through the mist,
the mist that does not notice. Silence.
Faint glimmer of the lantern is the signal.

SECRETS ON THE WAY
HEMLIGHETER PÅ VÄGEN
(1958)

Solitary Swedish Houses

A mix-max of black spruce
and smoking moonbeams.
Here's the croft lying low
and not a sign of life.

Till the morning dew murmurs
and an old man opens
– with a shaky hand – his window
and lets out an owl.

Further off, the new building
stands steaming
with the laundry butterfly
fluttering at the corner

in the middle of a dying wood
where the mouldering reads
through spectacles of sap
the proceedings of the bark-drillers.

Summer with flaxen-haired rain
or one solitary thunder-cloud
above a barking dog.
The seed is kicking inside the earth.

Agitated voices, faces
fly in the telephone wires
on stunted rapid wings
across the moorland miles.

The house on an island in the river
brooding on its stony foundations.
Perpetual smoke – they're burning
the forest's secret papers.

The rain wheels in the sky.
The light coils in the river.
Houses on the slope supervise
the waterfall's white oxen.

Autumn with a gang of starlings
holding dawn in check.
The people move stiffly
in the lamplight's theatre.

Let them feel without alarm
the camouflaged wings
and God's energy
coiled up in the dark.

The Man who Awoke with Singing over the Roofs

Morning. May-rain. The city is still quiet
as a mountain hamlet. The streets quiet. And in
the sky a bluish-green aero-engine rumbles. –
            The window is open.

The dream where the sleeper is lying prostrate
turns transparent. He stirs, begins
groping for attention's instruments –
            almost in space.

Weather Picture

The October sea glistens coldly
with its dorsal fin of mirages.

Nothing is left that remembers
the white dizziness of yacht races.

An amber glow over the village.
And all sounds in slow flight.

A dog's barking is a hieroglyph
painted in the air above the garden

where the yellow fruit outwits
the tree and drops of its own accord.

The Four Temperaments

The probing eye turns the sun's rays into police batons.
And in the evening: the hubbub from a party in the flat below
sprouts up through the floor like unreal flowers.

Driving on the plain. Darkness. The coach seemed stuck on the spot.
An anti-bird screeched in starry emptiness.
The albino sun stood over tossing dark seas.

                              *

A man like an uprooted tree with croaking foliage
and lightning at attention saw the beast-smelling
sun rise up among pattering wings on the world's

rocky island surging ahead behind banners of foam through night
and day with white sea-birds howling
on the deck and all with a ticket to Chaos.

                              *

You need only close your eyes to hear plainly
the gulls' faint Sunday over the sea's endless parish.
A guitar begins twanging in the thicket and the cloud dawdles

slowly as the green sledge of late spring
– with the whinnying light in the shafts –
comes gliding on the ice.

                              *

Woke with my girl's heels clopping in the dream
and outside two snowdrifts like winter's abandoned gloves
while leaflets from the sun cascaded over the city.

The road never comes to an end. The horizon rushes ahead.
The birds shake in the tree. The dust whirls round the wheels.
All the rolling wheels that contradict death!

Caprichos

It's getting dark in Huelva: sooty palm-trees
and the train whistle's flurrying
silver-white bats.

The streets have been filled up with people.
And the woman hurrying in the throng cautiously weighs
the last daylight on the balance of her eyes.

The office windows are open. You can still hear
how the horse is tramping in there.
The old horse with the rubber-stamp hooves.

Not till midnight are the streets empty.
At last in all the offices: it's blue.

Up there in space:
trotting silently, sparkling and black,
unseen and unbound,
having thrown its rider:
a new constellation I call 'The Horse'.

Siesta

The stones' Whitsun. And with sparkling tongues . . .
The city without weight in the midday hours.
Burials in simmering light. The drum which drowns
locked-in eternity's pounding fists.

The eagle rises and rises over the sleepers.
Sleep where the mill-wheel turns like thunder.
Tramping from the horse with blindfolded eyes.
Locked-in eternity's pounding fists.

The sleepers hang like weights in the tyrants' clock.
The eagle drifts dead in the sun's streaming white current.
And echoing in time – as in Lazarus' coffin –
locked-in eternity's pounding fists.

Izmir at Three O'Clock

Just ahead in the almost empty street
two beggars, one without legs –
he's carried on the other one's back.

They stood – as on a midnight road an animal
stands blinded staring into the carlights –
for one moment before passing on

and scuttled across the street like boys
in a playground while the midday heat's
myriad of clocks ticked in space.

Blue flowed past on the waters, flickering.
Black crept and shrank, stared from stone.
White blew up to a storm in the eyes.

When three o'clock was tramped under hooves
and darkness pounded in the wall of light
the city lay crawling at the sea's door

gleaming in the vulture's telescopic sight.

Secrets on the Way

Daylight struck the face of a man who slept.
His dream was more vivid
but he did not awake.

Darkness struck the face of a man who walked
among the others in the sun's strong
impatient rays.

It was suddenly dark, like a downpour.
I stood in a room that contained every moment –
a butterfly museum.

And the sun still as strong as before.
Its impatient brushes were painting the world.

Tracks

2 a.m.: moonlight. The train has stopped
out in the middle of the plain. Far away, points of light in a town,
flickering coldly at the horizon.

As when someone has gone into a dream so deep
he'll never remember having been there
when he comes back to his room.

As when someone has gone into an illness so deep
everything his days were becomes a few flickering points, a swarm,
cold and tiny at the horizon.

The train is standing quite still.
2 a.m.: bright moonlight, few stars.

Kyrie

Sometimes my life opened its eyes in the dark.
A feeling as if crowds drew through the streets
in blindness and anxiety on the way towards a miracle,
while I invisibly remain standing.

As the child falls asleep in terror
listening to the heart's heavy tread.
Slowly, slowly until morning puts its rays in the locks
and the doors of darkness open.

A Man from Benin
*(on a photograph of a 15th century relief in bronze
from the Negro state of Benin, showing a Portuguese Jew)*

When darkness fell I was still
but my shadow pounded
against the drumskin of hopelessness.
When the pounding began to ease
I saw the image of an image
of a man coming forward
in the emptiness, a page
lying open.
Like going past a house
long since abandoned
and someone appears at the window.
A stranger. He was the navigator.

He seemed to take notice.
Came nearer without a step.
In a hat which moulded itself
imitating our hemisphere
with the brim at the equator.
The hair parted in two fins.
The beard hung curled
round his mouth like eloquence.
He held his right arm bent.
It was thin like a child's.
The falcon that should have had its place
on his arm grew out
from his features.
He was the ambassador.
Interrupted in the middle of a speech
which the silence continues
even more forcibly.
Three peoples were silent in him.
He was the image of three peoples.
A Jew from Portugal,
who sailed away with the others,
the drifting and the waiting ones,
the hunched up flock
in the caravelle which was
their rocking wooden mother.
Landfall in a strange air
which made the atmosphere furry.
Observed in the market-place
by the negro cast-maker.
Long in his eyes' quarantine.
Reborn in the race of metal:
'I am come to meet him
who raises his lantern
to see himself in me.'

Balakirev's Dream
(1905)

The black grand piano, the gleaming spider
trembled at the centre of its net of music.

In the concert hall a land was conjured up
where stones were no heavier than dew.

But Balakirev dozed off during the music
and dreamed a dream about the tsar's droshky.

It rumbled over the cobblestones
straight into the crow-cawing blackness.

He sat alone inside the cab and looked
and also ran alongside on the road.

He knew the journey had lasted long
and his watch showed years, not hours.

There was a field where the plough lay
and the plough was a fallen bird.

There was an inlet where the vessel lay
ice-bound, lights out, with people on deck.

The droshky glided there across the ice
and the wheels spun with a sound of silk.

A lesser battleship: 'Sebastopol.'
He was aboard. The crew gathered round.

'You won't die if you can play.'
They showed a curious instrument.

Like a tuba, or a phonograph,
or a part of some unknown machine.

Stiff with fear and helpless he knew: it is
the instrument that drives the man-of-war.

He turned towards the nearest sailor,
made signs despairingly and begged:

'Cross yourself, like me, cross yourself!'
The sailor stared sadly like a blind man,

stretched out his arms, sank his head –
he hung as if nailed in the air.

The drums beat. The drums beat. Applause!
Balakirev wakened from his dream.

The wings of applause pattered in the hall.
He saw the man at the grand piano rise.

Outside the streets lay darkened by the strike.
The droshkies were rushing through the dark.

After an Attack

The sick boy.
Locked in a vision
with his tongue stiff as a horn.

He sits with his back turned to the picture of the cornfield.
The bandage round his jaw hinting at embalming.
His glasses are thick like a diver's. And everything is unanswered
and vehement like the telephone ringing in the dark.

But the picture behind him – a landscape that gives peace though the
          grain is a golden storm.
Sky like blue-weed and drifting clouds. Beneath in the yellow surge
some white shirts are sailing: reapers – they cast no shadows.

There's a man standing far across the field and he seems to be looking
     this way.
A broad hat darkens his face.
He seems to be observing the dark figure here in the room, perhaps
    to help.
Imperceptibly the picture has begun widening and opening behind the
    sick brooding
invalid. It sparks and pounds. Every grain is ablaze to rouse him!
The other – in the corn – gives a sign.

He has come close.
No one notices.

The Journey's Formulae
(from the Balkans, 1955)

1

A murmur of voices behind the ploughman.
He doesn't look round. The empty fields.
A murmur of voices behind the ploughman.
One by one the shadows break loose
and plunge into the summer sky's abyss.

2

Four oxen come, under the sky.
Nothing proud about them. And the dust thick
as wool. The insects' pens scrape.

A swirl of horses, lean as in
grey allegories of the plague.
Nothing gentle about them. And the sun raves.

3

The stable-smelling village with thin dogs.
The party official in the market square
in the stable-smelling village with white houses.

His heaven accompanies him: it is high
and narrow like inside a minaret.
The wing-trailing village on the hillside.

4

An old house has shot itself in the forehead.
Two boys kick a ball in the twilight.
A swarm of rapid echoes. – Suddenly, starlight.

5

On the road in the long darkness. My wristwatch
gleams obstinately with time's imprisoned insect.

The quiet in the crowded compartment is dense.
In the darkness the meadows stream past.

But the writer is halfway into his image, there
he travels, at the same time eagle and mole.

THE HALF-FINISHED HEAVEN
DEN HALVFÄRDIGA HIMLEN
(1962)

The Couple

They switch off the light and its white shade
glimmers for a moment before dissolving
like a tablet in a glass of darkness. Then up.
The hotel walls rise into the black sky.

The movements of love have settled, and they sleep
but their most secret thoughts meet as when
two colours meet and flow into each other
on the wet paper of a schoolboy's painting.

It is dark and silent. But the town has pulled closer
tonight. With quenched windows. The houses have approached.
They stand close up in a throng, waiting,
a crowd whose faces have no expressions.

The Tree and the Sky

There's a tree walking around in the rain,
it rushes past us in the pouring grey.
It has an errand. It gathers life
out of the rain like a blackbird in an orchard.

When the rain stops so does the tree.
There it is, quiet on clear nights
waiting as we do for the moment
when the snowflakes blossom in space.

Face to Face

In February living stood still.
The birds flew unwillingly and the soul
chafed against the landscape as a boat
chafes against the pier it lies moored to.

The trees stood with their backs turned towards me.
The deep snow was measured with dead straws.
The footprints grew old out on the crust.
Under a tarpaulin language pined.

One day something came to the window.
Work was dropped, I looked up.
The colours flared. Everything turned round.
The earth and I sprang towards each other.

Ringing

And the thrush blew its song on the bones of the dead.
We stood under a tree and felt time sinking and sinking.
The churchyard and the schoolyard met and widened into each other
        like two streams in the sea.

The ringing of the churchbells rose to the four winds borne by the
        gentle leverage of gliders.
It left behind a mightier silence on earth
and a tree's calm steps, a tree's calm steps.

Through the Wood

A place called Jacob's marsh
is the summer day's cellar
where the light sours to a drink
tasting of old age and slums.

The feeble giants stand entangled
closely – so nothing can fall.
The cracked birch moulders there
in an upright position like a dogma.

From the bottom of the wood I rise.
It grows light between the trunks.
It is raining over my roofs.
I am a water-spout for impressions.

At the edge of the wood the air is warm.
Great spruce, turned away and dark
whose muzzle hidden in the earth's mould
drinks the shadow of a shower.

November with Nuances of Noble Fur

It is the sky's being so grey
that makes the ground begin to shine:
the meadows with their timid green,
the ploughed fields dark as black-bread.

There is the red wall of a barn.
And there are acres under water
like shining rice-paddies in an Asia –
the gulls stand there reminiscing.

Misty spaces deep in the woods
chiming softly against each other.
Inspiration that lives secluded
and flees among the trees like Nils Dacke.

The Journey

In the underground station.
A crowding among placards
in a staring dead light.

The train came and collected
faces and portfolios.

Darkness next. We sat
in the carriages like statues,
hauled through the caverns.
Restraint, dreams, restraint.

In stations under sea-level
they sold the news of the dark.
People in motion sadly
silently under the clock-dials.

The train carried
outer garments and souls.

Glances in all directions
on the journey through the mountain.
Still no change.

But nearer the surface a murmuring
of bees began – freedom.
We stepped out of the earth.

The land beat its wings
once and became still
under us, widespread and green.

Ears of corn blew in
over the platforms.

Terminus – I
followed on, further.

How many were with me? Four,
five, hardly more.

Houses, roads, skies,
blue inlets, mountains
opened their windows.

C Major

When he came down to the street after the rendezvous
the air was swirling with snow.
Winter had come
while they lay together.
The night shone white.
He walked quickly with joy.
The whole town was downhill.
The smiles passing by –
everyone was smiling behind turned-up collars.
It was free!
And all the question-marks began singing of God's being.
So he thought.

A music broke out
and walked in the swirling snow
with long steps.
Everything on the way towards the note C.
A trembling compass directed at C.
One hour higher than the torments.
It was easy!
Behind turned-up collars everyone was smiling.

Noon Thaw

The morning air delivered its letters with stamps which glowed.
The snow shone and all burdens lightened – a kilo weighed just 700
        grammes.

The sun was high over the ice hovering on the spot both warm and cold.
The wind came out gently as if it were pushing a pram.

Families came out, they saw open sky for the first time in ages.
We found ourselves in the first chapter of a very gripping story.

The sunshine stuck to all the fur caps like pollen on bees
and the sunshine stuck to the name WINTER and stayed there till winter
        was over.

A still-life of logs on the snow made me thoughtful. I asked them:
'Are you coming along to my childhood?' They answered 'Yes.'

In among the copses there was a murmuring of words in a new language:
the vowels were blue sky and the consonants were black twigs and the
        speech was soft over the snow.

But the jet plane curtsying in its skirts of noise
made the silence on earth even stronger.

When We Saw the Islands Again

As the boat out there draws near
a sudden downpour makes it blind.
Quicksilver shot bounces on the water.
The blue-grey lies down.

The sea's there in the cottages too.
A stream of light in the dark hallway.
Heavy steps upstairs
and chests with newly-ironed smiles.
An Indian orchestra of copper pans.
A baby with eyes all at sea.

(The rain starts disappearing.
The smoke takes a few faltering steps
in the air above the roofs.)

Here comes more
bigger than dreams.

The beach with the hovels of elms.
A notice with the word CABLE.
The old heathery moor shines
for someone who comes flying.

Behind the rocks rich furrows
and the scarecrow our outpost
beckoning the colours to itself.

An always bright surprise
when the island reaches out a hand
and pulls me up from sadness.

From the Mountain

I stand on the mountain and look across the bay.
The boats rest on the surface of summer.
'We are sleepwalkers. Moons adrift.'
So say the white sails.

'We slip through a sleeping house.
We gently open the doors.
We lean towards freedom.'
So say the white sails.

Once I saw the wills of the world sailing.
They held the same course – one single fleet.
'We are dispersed now. No one's escort.'
So say the white sails.

Espresso

The black coffee they serve out of doors
among tables and chairs gaudy as insects.

Precious distillations
filled with the same strength as Yes and No.

It's carried out from the gloomy kitchen
and looks into the sun without blinking.

In the daylight a dot of beneficent black
that quickly flows into a pale customer.

It's like the drops of black profoundness
sometimes gathered up by the soul,

giving a salutary push: Go!
Inspiration to open your eyes.

The Palace

We stepped in. A single vast hall,
silent and empty, where the surface of the floor lay
like an abandoned skating rink.
All doors shut. The air grey.

Paintings on the walls. We saw
pictures throng lifelessly: shields, scale-
pans, fishes, struggling figures
in a deaf and dumb world on the other side.

A sculpture was set out in the void:
in the middle of the hall alone a horse stood
but at first when we were absorbed
by all the emptiness we did not notice him.

Fainter than the breathing in a shell
sounds and voices from the town
circling in this desolate space
murmuring and seeking power.

Also something else. Something darkly
set itself at our senses' five
thresholds without stepping over them.
Sand ran in every silent glass.

It was time to move. We walked
over to the horse. It was gigantic,
dark as iron. An image of power itself
abandoned when the princes left.

The horse spoke: 'I am The Only One.
The emptiness that rode me I have thrown.
This is my stable. I am growing quietly.
And I eat the silence that's in here.'

Syros

In Syros harbour left-over cargo steamers lay waiting.
Prow by prow by prow. Moored many years since:
CAPE RION, Monrovia.
KRITOS, Andros.
SCOTIA, Panama.

Dark pictures on the water, they have been hung away.

Like toys from our childhood which have grown to giants
and accuse us
of what we never became.

XELATROS, Pireus.
CASSIOPEIA, Monrovia.
The sea has read them through.

But the first time we came to Syros, it was at night,
we saw prow by prow by prow in the moonlight and thought:
what a mighty fleet, magnificent connections.

In the Nile Delta

The young wife wept over her food
in the hotel after a day in the city
where she saw the sick creep and huddle
and children bound to die of want.

She and her husband went to their room.
Sprinkled water to settle the dirt.
Lay on their separate beds with few words.
She fell in a deep sleep. He lay awake.

Out in the darkness a great noise ran past.
Murmurs, tramping, cries, carts, songs.
All in want. Never came to a stop.
And he sank in sleep curled in a No.

A dream came. He was on a voyage.
In the grey water a movement swirled
and a voice said: 'There is one who is good.
There is one who can see all without hating.'

A Dark Swimming Figure

About a prehistoric painting
on a rock in the Sahara:
a dark swimming figure
in an old river which is young.

Without weapons or strategy,
neither at rest nor quick
and cut from his own shadow
gliding on the bed of the stream.

He struggled to make himself free
from a slumbering green picture,
to come at last to the shore
and be one with his own shadow.

Lament

He laid aside his pen.
It rests still on the table.
It rests still in the empty room.
He laid aside his pen.

Too much that can neither be written nor kept silent!
He is paralysed by something happening far away
although the wonderful travelling-bag throbs like a heart.

Outside it is early summer.
From the greenery come whistlings – men or birds?
And cherry trees in bloom embrace the lorries which have come home.

Weeks go by.
Night comes slowly.
The moths settle on the window pane:
small pale telegrams from the world.

Allegro

I play Haydn after a black day
and feel a simple warmth in my hands.

The keys are willing. Soft hammers strike.
The resonance green, lively and calm.

The music says freedom exists
and someone doesn't pay the emperor tax.

I push down my hands in my Haydnpockets
and imitate a person looking on the world calmly.

I hoist the Haydnflag – it signifies:
'We don't give in. But want peace.'

The music is a glass-house on the slope
where the stones fly, the stones roll.

And the stones roll right through
but each pane stays whole.

The Half-Finished Heaven

Despondency breaks off its course.
Anguish breaks off its course.
The vulture breaks off its flight.

The eager light streams out,
even the ghosts take a draught.

And our paintings see daylight,
our red beasts of the ice-age studios.

Everything begins to look around.
We walk in the sun in hundreds.

Each man is a half-open door
leading to a room for everyone.

The endless ground under us.

The water is shining among the trees.

The lake is a window into the earth.

Nocturne

I drive through a village at night, the houses rise up
in the glare of my headlights – they're awake, want to drink.
Houses, barns, signs, ownerless dogs – it's now
they clothe themselves in Life. – The people are sleeping:

some can sleep peacefully, others have drawn features
as if training hard for eternity.
They don't dare let go though their sleep is heavy.
They rest like lowered crossing-barriers when the mystery draws past.

Outside the village the road goes far among the forest trees.
And the trees the trees keeping silence in concord with each other.
They have a theatrical colour, like firelight.
How distinct each leaf! They follow me right home.

I lie down to sleep, I see strange pictures
and signs scribbling themselves behind my eyelids
on the wall of the dark. Into the slit between wakefulness and dream
a large letter tries to push itself in vain.

A Winter Night

The storm puts its mouth to the house
   and blows to produce a note.
I sleep uneasily, turn, with shut eyes
   read the storm's text.

But the child's eyes are large in the dark
   and for the child the storm howls.
Both are fond of lamps that swing.
   Both are halfway towards speech.

The storm has childish hands and wings.
   The Caravan bolts towards Lapland.
And the house feels its own constellation of nails
   holding the walls together.

The night is calm over our floor
   (where all expired footsteps
rest like sunk leaves in a pond)
   but outside the night is wild.

Over the world goes a graver storm.
   It sets its mouth to our soul
And blows to produce a note. We dread
   that the storm will blow us empty.

BELLS AND TRACKS
KLANGER OCH SPÅR
(1966)

Portrait with Commentary

Here is a portrait of a man I knew.
He's sitting at the table, his newspaper open.
The eyes settle down behind the glasses.
The suit is washed with the shimmer of pinewoods.

It's a pale and half-complete face. –
Yet he always inspired trust. Which is why
people would hesitate to come near him
for fear of meeting some misfortune.

His father earned money like dew.
But no one felt secure there at home –
always a feeling that alien thoughts
broke into the house at night.

The newspaper, that big dirty butterfly,
the chair and the table and the face are at rest.
Life has stopped in big crystals.
But may it stop there only till further notice!

                          *

That which is I in him is at rest.
It exists. He doesn't notice
and therefore it lives, exists.

What am I? Now and then long ago
I came for a few seconds quite close
to ME, to ME, to ME.

But the moment I caught sight of ME
I lost ME – there was only a hole
through which I fell like Alice.

Lisbon

In the Alfama quarter the yellow tramcars sang on the steep slopes.
There were two prisons. One was for thieves.
They waved through the grilled windows.
They shouted that they wanted to be photographed.

'But here,' said the conductor giggling like a split man
'here sit politicians.' I saw the façade the façade the façade
and high up in a window a man
who stood with a telescope to his eye and looked out over the sea.

Laundry hung in blue. The walls were hot.
The flies read microscopic letters.
Six years later I asked a woman from Lisbon:
'Is it true, or have I dreamt it?'

From an African Diary
(1963)

On the Congolese market-place pictures
shapes move thin as insects, deprived of their human power.
It's a hard passage between two ways of life.
He who has gone furthest has a long way to go.

A young man found a foreigner lost among the huts.
Didn't know whether to take him for a friend or a subject for extortion.
His doubt disturbed him. They parted in confusion.

The Europeans mostly stay clustered round the car as if it were Mamma.
The crickets are as strong as electric shavers. The car drives home.
Soon the beautiful darkness comes, taking charge of the dirty clothes.
        Sleep.
He who has gone furthest has a long way to go.

It helps perhaps with hand-shakes like a flight of migratory birds.
It helps perhaps to let the truth out of the books.
It is necessary to go further.

The student reads in the night, reads and reads to be free
and having passed his exam he becomes a step for the next man.
A hard passage.
He who has gone furthest has a long way to go.

Crests

With a sigh the lifts begin to rise
in high blocks delicate as porcelain.
It will be a hot day out on the asphalt.
The traffic signs have drooping eyelids.

The land a steep slope to the sky.
Crest after crest, no proper shadow.
We fly there on the hunt for You
through the summer in cinemascope.

And in the evening I lie like a ship
with lights out, just at the right distance
from reality, while the crew
swarm in the parks there ashore.

Hommages

Walked along the antipoetic wall.
Die Mauer. Don't look over.
It wants to surround our adult lives
in the routine city, the routine landscape.

Éluard touched some button
and the wall opened
and the garden showed itself.

I used to go with the milk pail through the wood.
Purple trunks on all sides.
An old joke hung in there
as beautiful as a votive ship.

Summer read out of *Pickwick Papers*.
The good life, a tranquil carriage
crowded with excited gentlemen.

Close your eyes, change horses.

In distress come childish thoughts.
We sat by the sickbed and prayed
for a pause in the terror, a breach
where the Pickwicks could pull in.

Close your eyes, change horses.

It is easy to love fragments
that have been on the way a long time.
Inscriptions on church bells
and proverbs written across saints
and many-thousand-year-old seeds.

Archilochos! – No answer.

The birds roamed over the seas' rough pelt.
We locked ourselves in with Simenon
and felt the smell of human life
where the serials debouch.

Feel the smell of truth.

The open window has stopped
in front of the treetops here
and the evening sky's farewell letter.

Shiki, Björling and Ungaretti
with life's chalks on death's blackboard.
The poem which is completely possible.

I looked up when the branches swung.
White gulls were eating black cherries.

Winter's Formulae

1

I fell asleep in my bed
and woke up under the keel.

At four o'clock in the morning
when life's clean picked bones
coldly associate with each other.

I fell asleep among the swallows
and woke up among the eagles.

2

In the lamplight the ice on the road
is gleaming like lard.

This is not Africa.
This is not Europe.
This is nowhere other than 'here'.

And that which was 'I'
is only a word
in the December dark's mouth.

3

The institute's pavilions
displayed in the dark
shine like TV screens.

A hidden tuning-fork
in the great cold
sends out its tone.

I stand under the starry sky
and feel the world creep
in and out of my coat
as in an ant-hill.

4

Three dark oaks sticking out of the snow.
So gross, but nimble-fingered.
Out of their giant bottles
the greenery will bubble in spring.

5

The bus crawls through the winter evening.
It glimmers like a ship in the spruce forest
where the road is a narrow deep dead canal.

Few passengers: some old and some very young.
If it stopped and quenched the lights
the world would be deleted.

Morning Birds

I waken the car
whose windscreen is coated with pollen.
I put on my sunglasses.
The birdsong darkens.

Meanwhile another man buys a paper
at the railway station
close to a large goods wagon
which is all red with rust
and stands flickering in the sun.

No blank space anywhere here.

Straight through the spring warmth a cold corridor
where someone comes running
and tells how up at head office
they slandered him.

Through a back door in the landscape
comes the magpie
black and white.
And the blackbird darting to and fro
till everything becomes a charcoal drawing,
except the white clothes on the washing-line:
a palestrina chorus.

No blank space anywhere here.

Fantastic to feel how my poem grows
while I myself shrink.
It grows, it takes my place.
It pushes me aside.
It throws me out of the nest.
The poem is ready.

About History

1

One day in March I go down to the sea and listen.
The ice is as blue as the sky. It is breaking up under the sun.
The sun which also whispers in a microphone under the covering of
     ice.
It gurgles and froths. And someone seems to be shaking a sheet far
     out.
It's all like History: our Now. We are submerged, we listen.

2

Conferences like flying islands about to crash . . .
Then: a long trembling bridge of compromises.
There shall the whole traffic go, under the stars,
under the unborn pale faces,
outcast in the vacant spaces, anonymous as grains of rice.

3

Goethe travelled in Africa in '26 disguised as Gide and saw everything.
Some faces become clearer from everything they see after death.
When the daily news from Algeria was read out
there appeared a large house where all the windows were blacked,
all except one. And there we saw the face of Dreyfus.

4

Radical and Reactionary live together as in an unhappy marriage,
moulded by one another, dependent on one another.
But we who are their children must break loose.
Every problem cries in its own language.
Go like a bloodhound where the truth has trampled.

5

Out on the open ground not far from the buildings
an abandoned newspaper has lain for months, full of events.
It grows old through nights and days in rain and sun,
on the way to becoming a plant, a cabbage-head, on the way to being
        united with the earth.
Just as a memory is slowly transmuted into your own self.

.

Alone

I

One evening in February I came near to dying here.
The car skidded sideways on the ice, out
on the wrong side of the road. The approaching cars –
their lights – closed in.

My name, my girls, my job
broke free and were left silently behind
further and further away. I was anonymous
like a boy in a playground surrounded by enemies.

The approaching traffic had huge lights.
They shone on me while I pulled at the wheel
in a transparent terror that floated like egg white.
The seconds grew – there was space in them –
they grew as big as hospital buildings.

You could almost pause
and breathe out for a while
before being crushed.

Then something caught: a helping grain of sand
or a wonderful gust of wind. The car broke free
and scuttled smartly right over the road.
A post shot up and cracked – a sharp clang – it
flew away in the darkness.

Then – stillness. I sat back in my seat-belt
and saw someone coming through the whirling snow
to see what had become of me.

II

I have been walking for a long time
on the frozen Östergötland fields.
I have not seen a single person.

In other parts of the world
there are people who are born, live and die
in a perpetual crowd.

To be always visible – to live
in a swarm of eyes –
a special expression must develop.
Face coated with clay.

The murmuring rises and falls
while they divide up among themselves
the sky, the shadows, the sand grains.

I must be alone
ten minutes in the morning
and ten minutes in the evening.
– Without a programme.

Everyone is queuing at everyone's door.

Many.

One.

On the Outskirts of Work

In the middle of work
we start longing fiercely for wild greenery,
for the Wilderness itself, penetrated only
by the thin civilisation of the telephone wires.

                    *

The moon of leisure circles the planet Work
with its mass and weight. – That's how they want it.
When we are on the way home the ground pricks up its ears.
The underground listens to us via the grass-blades.

                    *

Even in this working day there is a private calm.
As in a smoky inland area where a canal flows:
THE BOAT appears unexpectedly in the traffic
or glides out behind the factory, a white vagabond.

                    *

One Sunday I walk past an unpainted new building
standing before a grey wet surface.
It is half finished. The wood has the same light colour
as the skin on someone bathing.

*

Outside the lamps the September night is totally dark.
When the eyes adjust, there is faint light
over the ground where large snails glide out
and the mushrooms are as numerous as the stars.

After Someone's Death

Once there was a shock
which left behind a long pale glimmering comet's tail.
It contains us. It makes TV pictures blurred.
It deposits itself as cold drops on the aerials.

You can still shuffle along on skis in the winter sun
among groves where last year's leaves still hang.
They are like pages torn from old telephone directories –
the subscribers' names are eaten up by the cold.

It is still beautiful to feel your heart throbbing.
But often the shadow feels more real than the body.
The samurai looks insignificant
beside his armour of black dragon-scales.

Oklahoma

1

The train stopped far south. There was snow in New York.
Here you could go about in shirtsleeves the whole night.
But no one was out. Only the cars
flew past in their glare, flying saucers.

2

'We battlefields who are proud
of our many dead . . .'
said a voice while I wakened.

The man behind the counter said:
'I'm not trying to sell it,
I'm not trying to sell it,
I only want you to look at it.'
And he showed the Indians' axes.

The boy said:
'I know I have a prejudice,
I don't want to be left with it sir.
What do you think of us?'

3

This motel is a strange shell. With a hired car
(a huge white servant outside the door)
almost without memory and without ploy
at last I can settle on my point of balance.

Summer Plain

We have seen so much.
Reality has used us up so much,
but here is summer at last:

a large airfield – the flight controller is bringing down
load after load of frozen
people from space.

The grass and the flowers – here we land.
The grass has a green manager.
I report myself.

Downpour over the Interior

The rain is hammering on the car roofs.
The thunder rumbles. The traffic slows down.
The lights are switched on in the middle of the summer day.

The smoke pours down the chimneys.
All living things huddle, shut their eyes.
A movement inwards, feel life stronger.

The car is almost blind. He stops
lights a private fire and smokes
while the water swills along the windows.

Here on a forest road, winding and out of the way
near a lake with water lilies
and a long mountain that vanishes in the rain.

Up there lie the piles of stones
from the iron age when this was a place
for tribal wars, a colder Congo

and the danger drove beasts and men together
to a murmuring refuge behind the walls,
behind thickets and stones on the hilltop.

A dark slope, someone moving
up clumsily with his shield on his back
– this he imagines while his car is standing.

It begins to lighten, he winds down the window.
A bird flutes away to itself
in a thinning silent rain.

The lake surface is taut. The thunder-sky whispers
down through the water lilies to the mud.
The forest windows are slowly opening.

But the thunder strikes out of the stillness!
A deafening clap. And then a void
where the last drops fall.

In the silence he hears an answer coming.
From far away. A kind of coarse child's voice.
It rises, a bellowing from the hill.

A roar of mingled notes.
A long-hoarse trumpet from the iron age.
Perhaps from inside himself.

Under Pressure

The blue sky's engine-drone is deafening.
We're living here on a shuddering work-site
where the ocean depths can suddenly open up –
shells and telephones hiss.

You can see beauty only from the side, hastily.
The dense grain on the field, many colours in a yellow stream.
The restless shadows in my head are drawn there.
They want to creep into the grain and turn to gold.

Darkness falls. At midnight I go to bed.
The smaller boat puts out from the larger boat.
You are alone on the water.
Society's dark hull drifts further and further away.

Open and Closed Spaces

A man feels the world with his work like a glove.
He rests for a while at midday having laid aside the gloves on the shelf.
There they suddenly grow, spread
and black-out the whole house from inside.

The blacked-out house is away out among the winds of spring.
'Amnesty,' runs the whisper in the grass: 'amnesty.'
A boy sprints with an invisible line slanting up in the sky
where his wild dream of the future flies like a kite bigger than the
        suburb.

Further north you can see from a summit the blue endless carpet of
        pine forest
where the cloud shadows
are standing still.
No, are flying.

An Artist in the North

I Edvard Grieg moved like a free man among men.
Ready with a joke, read the papers, travelled here and there.
Led the orchestra.
The concert-hall with its lamps trembling in triumph like the train-ferry
        when it puts in.

I have brought myself up here to be shut in with silence.
My work-cottage is small.
The piano a tight fit like the swallow under the eaves.

For the most part the beautiful steep slopes say nothing.
There is no passageway
but sometimes a little hatch opens
and a strangely seeping light direct from trolldom.

Reduce!

And the hammer-blows in the mountain came
came
came
came one spring night into our room
disguised as beating of the heart.

The year before I die I'll send out four hymns to track down God.
But it starts here.
A song about what is near.

What is near.

The battlefield within us
where we the Bones of the Dead
fight to become living.

In the Open

1

Late autumn labyrinth.
At the entrance to the wood a discarded empty bottle.
Go in. This year the wood is silent abandoned halls.
Only a few kinds of noise: as if someone were removing twigs cautiously
            with tweezers
or a hinge creaking faintly inside a thick tree trunk.
The frost has breathed on the mushrooms and they have shrivelled.
They are like objects and garments found after a disappearance.
Now twilight comes. It's a matter of reaching out
and seeing your landmarks again: the rusty implement out on the field
and the house on the other side of the lake, a russet square strong
            as a bouillon cube.

2

A letter from America set me off, drove me out
one light night in June on the empty streets in the suburb
among newborn blocks without memory, cool as blueprints.

The letter in my pocket. Desperate furious striding, it is a kind of
        pleading.
With you, evil and good have real faces.
With us, it's mostly a struggle between roots, ciphers and shades of
        light.

Those who run death's errands don't avoid the daylight.
They rule from glass storeys. They swarm in the sun's blaze.
They lean across the counter and turn their heads.

Far away I happen to stop before one of the new façades.
Many windows all merging together into one single window.
The light of the night sky is caught there and the gliding of the
        treetops.
It is a mirroring sea without waves, erect in the summer night.

Violence seems unreal
for a little.

3

The sun scorches. The plane flies low
throwing a shadow in the form of a large cross rushing forward on the
        ground.
A man is crouching in the field at something.
The shadow comes.
For a fraction of a second he is in the middle of the cross.

I have seen the cross that hangs under cool church vaults.
Sometimes it's like a snapshot
of something in violent movement.

Slow Music

The building is closed. The sun crowds in through the windows
and warms up the surfaces of desks
that are strong enough to take the load of human fate.

We are outside, today, on the long wide slope.
Many have dark clothes. You can stand in the sun with your eyes shut
and feel yourself being slowly blown forward.

I come down to the water too seldom. But here I am now,
among large stones with peaceful backs.
Stones which slowly migrated backwards up out of the waves.

SEEING IN THE DARK
MÖRKERSEENDE
(1970)

The Name

I grow sleepy during the car journey and I drive in under the trees at
the side of the road. I curl up in the back seat and sleep. For how long?
Hours. Darkness had come on.

Suddenly I'm awake and don't know where I am. Wide-awake, but it
doesn't help. Where am I? WHO am I? I am something that wakens in
a back seat, twists about in panic like a cat in a sack. Who?

At last my life returns. My name comes like an angel. Outside the walls
a trumpet signal blows (as in the Leonora overture) and the rescuing
footsteps come smartly down the overlong stairway. It is I! It is I!

But impossible to forget the fifteen second struggle in the hell of oblivion,
a few metres from the main road, where the traffic glides past with its
lights on.

A Few Minutes

The squat pine in the swamp holds up its crown: a dark rag.
But what you see is nothing
compared to the roots, the widespread, secretly creeping, immortal or
          half-mortal
root system.

I you she he also branch out.
Outside what one wills.
Outside the Metropolis.

A shower falls out of the milk-white summer sky.
It feels as if my five senses were linked to another creature
which moves stubbornly
as the brightly-clad runners in a stadium where the darkness streams
          down.

Breathing Space July

The man lying on his back under the high trees
is up there too. He rills out in thousands of twigs,
sways to and fro,
sits in an ejector seat that releases in slow motion.

The man down by the jetties narrows his eyes at the water.
The jetties grow old more quickly than people.
They have silver grey timber and stones in their stomachs.
The blinding light beats right in.

The man travelling all day in an open boat
over the glittering straits
will sleep at last inside a blue lamp
while the islands creep like large moths across the glass.

By the River

Talking with contemporaries I saw heard behind their faces
the stream
that flowed and flowed and pulled with it the willing and the unwilling.

And the creature with stuck-together eyes that wants
to go right down the rapids with the current
throws itself forward without trembling
in a furious hunger for simplicity.

The water pulls more and more heavily

as where the river narrows and goes over
in the rapids – the place where I paused
after a journey through dry woods

one June evening: the radio gives the latest
on the special meeting: Kosygin, Eban.
A few thoughts drill despairingly.
A few people down in the village.

And under the suspension bridge the masses of water hurl
past. Here comes the timber. Some logs
shoot right out like torpedoes. Others turn
cross-wise, twirl sluggishly and helplessly away

and some nose against the river banks,
push among stones and rubbish, wedge fast
and pile up there like clasped hands

motionless in the uproar . . .

              I saw heard from the bridge
in a cloud of mosquitoes,
together with some boys. Their bicycles
buried in the greenery – only the horns
stuck up.

Outskirts

Men in overalls the same colour as the earth come up out of a ditch.
It is an intermediate place, stale-mate, neither city nor country.
The high cranes on the horizon want to take the great leap but the
        clocks don't want to.
Cement pipes, scattered around, lick up the light with dry tongues.
Car-body repair shops in one-time barns.
The stones throw their shadows abruptly like objects on the surface
        of the moon.
And these places just multiply.
Like what they bought with Judas' money: 'the potter's field, to bury
        strangers in'.

Traffic

The long-distance lorry with its trailer crawls through the mist
and is a large shadow of the dragonfly larva
which stirs in the mud of the lake-bed.

Headlights meet in a dripping forest.
One can't see the other's face.
The flood of light pours through the needles.

We come shadows vehicles from all directions
in the twilight, drive together behind each other
past each other, glide forward in a muffled clamour

out onto the plain where factories brood
and the buildings sink two millimetres
each year – the ground is eating them slowly.

Unidentified paws set their marks
on the brightest products dreamt up here.
The seeds try to live in the asphalt.

But first the chestnut trees, gloomy as if
they prepared a blossoming of iron gloves
instead of white clusters, and behind them

the company office – a faulty strip-light
blinks blinks. There's a secret door here. Unlock it –
look into the inverted periscope

downwards, to the openings, to the deep tubes
where the algae grow like the beards of the dead
and the Cleaner drifts in his dress of slime

with feebler and feebler strokes, on the point of suffocating.
And no one knows what will happen, only that the chain
perpetually breaks, perpetually joins together again.

Night Duty

1

Tonight I am down among the ballast.
I am one of the silent weights
which prevent the ship overturning!
Obscure faces in the darkness like stones.
They can only hiss: 'don't touch me'.

2

Other voices throng, the listener
glides like a lean shadow over the radio's
luminous band of stations.
The language marches in step with the executioners.
Therefore we must get a new language.

3

The wolf is here, friend for every hour
touching the windows with his tongue.
The valley is full of crawling axe-handles.
The night-flyer's din pours over the sky
sluggishly, like a wheel-chair with iron rims.

4

They are digging up the town. But it is silent now.
Under the elms in the churchyard:
an empty excavator. The scoop against the earth –
the gesture of a man who has fallen asleep at table
with his fist in front of him. – Bell-ringing.

The Open Window

I stood shaving one morning
before the open window
one storey up.
I switched the shaver on.
It began to purr.
It buzzed louder and louder.
It grew to an uproar.
It grew to a helicopter
and a voice – the pilot's – penetrated
through the din, shrieked:
'Keep your eyes open!
You're seeing all this for the last time.'
We rose.
Flew low over the summer.
So many things I liked, have they any weight?
Dozens of dialects of green.
And especially the red in the wooden house walls.
The beetles glistened in the dung, in the sun.
Cellars which were pulled up by the roots
came through the air.
Activity.
The printing-presses crawled.
Just now the people were
the only things that were still.
They observed a minute's silence.
And especially the dead in the country churchyard
were still
as if sitting for a picture in the infancy of the camera.
Fly low!
I didn't know where I
turned my head –
with a double field of vision
like a horse.

Preludes

1

I shy at something which comes shuffling cross-wise in the sleet.
Fragment of what will happen.
A wall broken loose. Something without eyes. Hard.
A face of teeth!
A solitary wall. Or is the house there
although I don't see it?
The future: an army of empty houses
picking its way forward in the sleet.

2

Two truths draw nearer each other. One comes from inside, one comes
        from outside
and where they meet we have a chance to see ourselves.

He who notices what is happening cries despairingly: 'Stop!
whatever you like, if only I avoid knowing myself.'

And there is a boat which wants to put in – it tries just here –
thousands of times it comes and tries.

Out of the forest gloom comes a long boat-hook, it is pushed in through
        the open window,
in among the party guests who danced themselves warm.

3

The flat where I lived the greater part of my life is to be cleared out.
It is now quite empty. The anchor has let go – although we are still
mourning it is the lightest flat in the whole city. The truth needs no
furniture. I have made a journey round life and come back to the starting-
point: a blown-out room. Things I have taken part in here show on the
walls like Egyptian paintings, scenes on the inside of a burial chamber.
But they are steadily being erased. For the light is too strong. The
windows have become bigger. The empty flat is a large telescope aimed
at the sky. It is silent as a quaker service. What can be heard are the
back-yard pigeons, their cooing.

Upright

In a moment of concentration I succeeded in catching the hen, I stood with it in my hands. Curiously, it did not feel properly alive: stiff, dry, an old white feather-trimmed woman's hat, which cried out truths from 1912. Thunder hung in the air. From the wooden planks a scent rose as when you open a photo album so aged that you can no longer identify the portraits.

I carried the hen into the enclosure and let her go. Suddenly she was very much alive, knew where she was and ran according to the rules. The hen-yard is full of taboos. But the earth around is full of love and tenacity. A low stone wall half overgrown with greenery. When dusk comes the stones begin to gleam faintly with the hundred-year-old warmth from the hands that built.

The winter has been hard but now summer is here and the earth wants to have us upright. Free but wary, as when you stand up in a slim boat. A memory from Africa occurs to me: on the shore at Chari, many boats, a very friendly atmosphere, the almost blue-black people with three parallel scars on each cheek (the SARA tribe). I am welcomed aboard – a canoe of dark wood. It is surprisingly rickety, also when I squat down. A balancing act. If the heart lies on the left side you must incline your head a little to the right, nothing in the pockets, no large gestures, all rhetoric must be left behind. Just this: rhetoric is impossible here. The canoe glides out on the water.

The Bookcase

It was fetched from the dead woman's apartment. It stood empty for a few days, empty, until I filled it with books, all the bound ones, the heavy ones. In doing so, I had let in the nether world. Something came from underneath, rose slowly and inexorably like a massive column of mercury. One was not allowed to turn one's head away.

The dark volumes, closed faces. They are like Algerians who stood at the Friedrichstrasse checkpoint and waited for the Volkspolizei to examine their passports. My own passport has long since lain among the glass cages. And the haze which was in Berlin in those days is also inside the bookcase. In there lies an old despair that tastes of Passchendaele and the Versailles Peace, that tastes even older. The dark heavy tomes – I come back to them – they are in reality a kind of passport and they are so thick because they have collected so many stamps through the centuries. Evidently you cannot travel with enough heavy baggage, now when you set off, when you at last . . .

All the old historians are there, they rise up there and look into our family. Nothing is heard but the lips are moving all the time behind the glass ('Passchendaele' . . .). It makes you think of an aged civil service department (a pure ghost-story follows), a building where portraits of long since dead men hang behind glass and one morning there was vapour on the inside of the glass. They had begun to breathe during the night.

The bookcase is still more powerful. The glances straight across the border! A gleaming membrane, the gleaming membrane on a dark river which the room must see itself in. And one is not allowed to turn one's head away.

PATHS
STIGAR
(1973)

To Friends behind a Frontier

1

I wrote so meagrely to you. But what I couldn't write
swelled and swelled like an old-fashioned airship
and drifted away at last through the night sky.

2

The letter is now at the censor's. He lights his lamp.
In the glare my words fly up like monkeys on a grille,
rattle it, stop, and bare their teeth.

3

Read between the lines. We'll meet in 200 years
when the microphones in the hotel walls are forgotten
and can at last sleep, become trilobites.

From the Thaw of 1966

Headlong headlong waters; roaring; old hypnosis.
The river swamps the car-cemetery, glitters
behind the masks.
I hold tight to the bridge railing.
The bridge: a big iron bird sailing past death.

Sketch in October

The tug is freckled with rust. What's it doing here so far inland?
It's a heavy extinguished lamp in the cold.
But the trees have wild colours: signals to the other shore.
As if someone wanted to be fetched.

On my way home I see mushrooms sprouting through the grass.
They are the fingers, stretching for help, of someone
who has for long sobbed alone in the darkness down there.
We are the earth's.

Further In

On the main road into the city
when the sun is low.
The traffic thickens, crawls.
It is a sluggish dragon glittering.
I am one of the dragon's scales.
Suddenly the red sun is
right in the middle of the windscreen
streaming in.
I am transparent
and writing becomes visible
inside me
words in invisible ink
which appear
when the paper is held to the fire!
I know I must get far away
straight through the city and then
further until it is time to go out
and walk far in the forest.
Walk in the footprints of the badger.
It gets dark, difficult to see.
In there on the moss lie stones.
One of the stones is precious.
It can change everything
it can make the darkness shine.
It is a switch for the whole country.
Everything depends on it.
Look at it, touch it . . .

The Outpost

I'm ordered out in a heap of stones
like a distinguished corpse from the iron age.
The others are back in the tent sleeping
stretched out like spokes in a wheel.

In the tent the stove rules: a big snake
that has swallowed a ball of fire and hisses.
But out in the spring night it is silent
among cold stones that are waiting for day.

Out there in the cold I begin to fly
like a shaman, I fly to her body
with its white marks from her bikini –
we were out in the sun. The moss was warm.

I flit over warm moments
but can't stop for long.
They're whistling me back through space –
I crawl out from the stones. Here and now.

Mission: to be where I am.
Even in that ridiculous, deadly serious
role – I am the place
where creation is working itself out.

Daybreak, the sparse tree-trunks
are coloured now, the frost-bitten
spring flowers form a silent search party
for someone who has vanished in the dark.

But to be where I am. And to wait.
I am anxious, stubborn, confused.
Coming events, they're there already!
I know it. They're outside:

a murmuring crowd outside the gate.
They can pass only one by one.
They want in. Why? They're coming
one by one. I am the turnstile.

Along the Radius

I

The ice-bound river is blazing with sun
here is the world's roof
silence.

I'm sitting on an upturned boat on the bank
swallowing the drug of silence
spinning gently.

II

A wheel spreads out endlessly, turns.
Here is the centre, almost
still.

Further out, perceptible movement: the steps in the snow
the writing which shuffles along
the façades.

The rumbling traffic on the highways
and the silent traffic
of ghosts.

And further out: the tragic masks in the head-wind
in the whine of speed – further out:
the rush

where the last words of love evaporate –
the drips that creep
on the steel wings –

profiles that cry out – the suspended head-phones
chatter at each other –
kamikaze!

III

The ice-bound river glitters and is silent.
The shadows lie deep here
and voiceless.

My steps here were explosions in the ground
which the silence paints over
paints over.

Looking through the Ground

The white sun is soaking through the smog.
The light drips, gropes its way down

to my deep-down eyes that are resting
deep under the city looking up

seeing the city from below: streets, foundations –
like aerial photos of a city in war

the wrong way round – a mole photo:
silent squares in sombre colours.

The decisions are taken there. No telling
bones of the dead from bones of the living.

The sunlight's volume is turned up,
it floods into flight-cabins and peapods.

December Evening 1972

Here I come, the invisible man, perhaps employed
by a Great Memory to live right now. And I am driving past

the locked-up white church – a wooden saint is standing in there
smiling, helpless, as if they had taken away his glasses.

He is alone. Everything else is now, now, now. The law of gravity
        pressing us
against our work by day and against our beds by night. The war.

The Dispersed Congregation

I

We made an effort, showing our homes.
The visitor thought: you live well.
The slum is within you.

II

Inside the church: vaults and columns
white as plaster, like the plaster bandage
round the broken arm of faith.

III

Inside the church: the begging bowl
that raises itself from the floor
and goes along the pews.

IV

But the church bells must go under the earth.
They hang in the sewage tunnels.
They toll under our steps.

V

The sleepwalker Nicodemus on his way
to the Address. Who has the address?
Don't know. But that's where we're going.

Late May

Apple trees and cherry trees in bloom help the town to soar
in the sweet dirty May night, white life-jacket, my thoughts range out.
Grasses and weeds with silent stubborn wing-beats.
The letter-box shines calmly, what's written can't be taken back.

Soft cool wind gets through my shirt and gropes for my heart.
Apple trees and cherry trees, they laugh silently at Solomon
they blossom in my tunnel. I need them
not to forget but to remember.

Elegy

I open the first door.
It's a large sunlit room.
A heavy car goes past in the street
and makes the porcelain tremble.

I open door number two.
Friends! You drank the darkness
and became visible.

Door number three. A narrow hotel-room.
Outlook on a back street.
A lamp sparking on the asphalt.
Beautiful slag of experiences.

BALTICS
ÖSTERSJÖAR
(1974)

I

It was before the age of the radio masts.

Grandfather was a new-made pilot. In the almanac he wrote down the
          vessels he piloted –
names, destinations, draught.
Examples from 1884:
Steamer Tiger Capt. Rowan 16 ft Hull Gefle Furusund
Brigg Ocean Capt. Andersen 8 ft Sandöfjord Hernösand Furusund
Steamer St Pettersburg Capt Libenberg 11 ft Stettin Libau Sandhamn

He took them out to the Baltic, through the marvellous labyrinth of
          islands and waters.
And those who met on board and were carried by the same hull for
          a few hours, or days,
how much did they come to know each other?
Conversations in misspelt English, understanding and misunderstanding
          but very little conscious falsehood.
How much did they come to know each other?

When it was thick fog: half-speed, half blind ahead. At one single stride
          the cape came out of the invisible and was right on them.
Every other minute a bellowing signal. His eyes read straight into the
          invisible.
(Had he the labyrinth in his head?)
The minutes passed.
Shallows and skerries he memorised like psalm verses.
And that feeling of we're-just-here which must be kept, like carrying
          a brimful pail without spilling a drop.

A glance down in the engine-room.
The compound machine long-lived as a human heart toiled with great
          supple bouncing movements, acrobats of steel, and the smells
          came up like out of a kitchen.

II

The wind is in the pine forest. Sighing heavily and lightly.
The Baltic is sighing in the middle of the island also, far within the
      forest you are out on the open sea.
The old woman hated the sighing in the trees. Her face stiffened in
      melancholy when the wind blew up:
'We must think about the men out in the boats.'
But she heard something else as well in the sighing, as I do, we are kin.
(We are walking together. She's been dead for thirty years.)
There's sighing, yes and no, understanding and misunderstanding.
There's sighing, three sound children, one in a sanatorium and two dead.
The great current that blows life into some flames and blows others
      out. The conditions.
Sighing: Save me, O God; for the waters are come in unto my soul.
You go on, listening, and then reach a point where the frontiers open
or rather
where everything becomes a frontier. An open place sunk in darkness.
      The people stream out from the faintly lit buildings round about.
      Murmuring.

A new breath of wind and the place lies desolate and silent again.

A new breath of wind, sighing about other shores.
It's about war.
It's about places where citizens are under control,
where their thoughts are made with emergency exits,
where a conversation between friends really becomes a test of what
      friendship means.
And when you are with people you don't know so well. Control.
      A certain sincerity is in place
if only you don't take your eyes off what's drifting on the outskirts
      of the conversation: something dark, a dark stain.
Something that can drift in
and destroy everything. Don't take your eyes off it!
What can we compare it to? A mine?
No, that would be too concrete. And almost too peaceful – for on our
      coast most of the stories about mines have a happy ending, the
      terror short-lived.
As in this story from the light-ship: 'In the autumn of 1915 we slept
      uneasily . . .' etc. A drift-mine was sighted

as it drifted slowly towards the light-ship, then sank and resurfaced,
      sometimes hidden by the waters, sometimes glimpsed like a
      spy in a crowd.
The crew were in a sweat and shot at it with rifles. No use. At last they
      put out a boat and made fast a long line to it and carefully and
      slowly towed it to the experts.
Afterwards they set up the dark shell of the mine in a sandy plantation
      as an ornament
together with the shells of Strombus Gigas from the West Indies.

And the sea wind is in the dry pines further away, hurrying over the
      churchyard sand,
past the leaning stones, the pilots' names.
The dry sighing
of great doors opening and great doors closing.

III

In the half-dark corner of a Gotland church, in a glimmer of soft mildew
there's a sandstone font – 12th century – the mason's name
is still there, shining out
like a row of teeth in a mass grave:
                    HEGWALDR
                                the name's left. And his pictures
here and on the sides of other pots, human swarms, figures stepping out
      of the stone.
There the eyes' kernels of good and evil are split.
Herod at table: the roasted cock flies up and crows 'Christus natus est'
      – the waiter was executed –
close by, the child is born, under clusters of faces dignified and helpless
      as those of young apes.
And the fleeing steps of the pious
echoing over dragon-scaled sewer openings.
(The images stronger in memory than when seen direct, strongest
when in memory the font turns like a slow rumbling merry-go-round).
Nowhere lee. Everywhere risk.
As it was. As it is.
Only in there is there peace, in the vessel's water that no one sees,

but on the outer walls the battle is raging.
And peace can come drop by drop, perhaps at night
when we know nothing
or when you are lying in a hospital ward on a drip.

People, beasts, ornaments.
There is no landscape. Ornaments.

Mr B, my amiable travelling companion, in exile,
escaped from Robben Island, says:
'I envy you. I feel nothing for nature.
But *figures in a landscape*, that says something to me.'

Here are figures in a landscape.
A photo from 1865. The steamer is at the pier in the sound.
Five figures. A lady in a bright crinoline, like a bell, like a flower.
The men are like extras in a rustic play.
They're all beautiful, irresolute, in the process of being rubbed out.
They step ashore for a little while. They're being rubbed out.
The steam launch is an extinct model –
high funnel, sunroof, narrow hull –
it's utterly foreign, a UFO that's landed.
Everything else in the photo is shockingly real:
the ripples on the water,
the opposite shore –
I can stroke my hand over the rough rock-faces,
I can hear the sighing in the spruces.
It's near. It's
today.
The waves are topical.

Now a hundred years later. The waves are coming in from no-man's
        water
and break on the stones.
I walk along the shore. Walking along the shore is not as it was.
You have to take in too much, keep up many conversations at once,
        you have thin walls.
Each thing has acquired a new shadow behind the usual shadow
and you hear it trailing along even in total darkness.

It's night.

The strategic planetarium rotates. The lenses stare in the dark.
The night sky is full of numbers and they are fed
into a twinkling cupboard
a piece of furniture
where there lives the energy of a locust swarm that denudes the acreage
    of Somaliland in half an hour.

I don't know if we are at the beginning or coming to the end.
The summing-up can't be done, the summing-up is impossible.
The summing-up is the mandrake –
(See the encyclopedia of superstitions:
                         MANDRAKE
                                        miracle-working plant
which when torn out of the ground gave off such an appalling scream
a man would drop dead. A dog had to do it.)

IV

From leeward,
close-ups.

Bladderwrack: The weed-forests shine in the clear water, they are
        young, you want to emigrate there, lie down full-length on your
        mirror image and sink to a certain depth – the weed that holds
        itself up with air-bladders as we hold ourselves up with ideas.

Bullhead: The fish who is a toad who wanted to become a butterfly and
        succeeded a third of the way, hides himself in the seaweed but
        is drawn up in the nets, hooked fast by his pathetic spikes and
        warts – when you disentangle it from the meshes your hands
        are gleaming with slime.

Rockface. Out on the sun-warmed lichens the insects scurry, they're
        in a rush like second-hands – the pine throws a shadow, it
        moves slowly like an hour-hand – inside me time stands still,
        endless with time, the time required to forget all languages and
        to discover perpetuum mobile.

On the lee-side you can hear the grass growing: a faint drumming from
        underneath, a faint roar of millions of little gas-flames, that's
        what it's like to hear the grass growing.

And now: the width of water, without doors, the open frontier
that grows broader and broader
the further you reach out.

There are days when the Baltic is a calm endless roof.
Dream your naive dreams then about someone coming crawling on the
        roof trying to sort out the flag-lines,
trying to hoist
the rag –

the flag which is so eroded by the wind and blackened by the funnels
        and bleached by the sun it can be everyone's.

But it's a long way to Liepaja.

V

July 30th. The strait has become eccentric – swarming with jellyfish
        today for the first time in years, they pump themselves forward
        calmly and patiently, they belong to the same line: *Aurelia*, they
        drift like flowers after a sea-burial, if you take them out of the
        water all their form vanishes, as when an indescribable truth
        is lifted out of silence and formulated to an inert mass, but they
        are untranslatable, they must stay in their own element.

August 2nd. Something wants to be said but the words don't agree.
Something which can't be said,
aphasia,
there are no words but perhaps a style . . .

You can wake up in the small hours
jot down a few words
on the nearest paper, a newsprint margin
(the words radiate meaning!)
but in the morning: the same words now say nothing, scrawls,
        slips-of-the-tongue.
Or fragments of the high nocturnal style that drew past?

Music comes to a man, he's a composer, he's played, makes a career,
        becomes Conservatory Director.
The climate changes, he's condemned by the authorities.
His pupil K. is set up as prosecutor.
He's threatened, degraded, removed.
After a few years the disgrace lessens, he's rehabilitated.
Then, cerebral haemorrhage: paralysis on the right side with aphasia,
        can grasp only short phrases, says the wrong words.
Beyond the reach of eulogy or execration.
But the music's left, he goes on composing in his own style,
for the rest of his days he becomes a medical sensation.

He wrote music to texts he no longer understood –
in the same way
we express something through our lives
in the humming chorus full of mistaken words.

The death-lectures went on for several terms. I attended
together with people I didn't know
(who are you?)
– then each went his own way, profiles.

I looked at the sky and at the earth and straight ahead
and since then I've been writing a long letter to the dead
on a typewriter with no ribbon just a horizon line
so the words knock in vain and nothing sticks.

I pause with my hand on the door-handle, take the pulse of the house.
The walls are so full of life
(the children don't dare to sleep alone in the little room upstairs –
        what makes me safe makes them uneasy).

August 3rd. Out there in the damp grass
a greeting shuffles from the Middle Ages, the Edible Snail,
subtle gleaming grey-and-yellow, with his house aslant,
implanted by monks who liked their *escargots* – the Franciscans were
        here,
broke stone and burned lime, the island became theirs in 1288, a gift
        of King Magnus
('Almes fordoth all wykkednes / And quenchyth synne and makyth
        hyt les')
the forest fell, the ovens burned, the chalk was sailed into the monastery
        buildings . . .

                    Sister snail
almost motionless in the grass, the antennae are sucked in
and rolled out, disturbances and hesitation . . .
How like myself in my searching!

The wind that's been blowing carefully all day
– the blades of grass on the outer skerries are all counted –
has lain down peacefully at the heart of the island. The match-flame
          stands straight.
The sea-painting and the forest-painting darken together.
The foliage on the five-storey trees turns black.
'Each summer is the last.' Empty words
for the creatures in the late summer midnight
where the crickets whirr their sewing-machines frantically
and the Baltic is close
and the lonely water-tap rises among the wild roses
like the statue of a horseman. The water tastes of iron.

VI

Grandmother's story before it's forgotten: her parents die young
father first. When the widow knows the disease will take her too
she walks from house to house, sails from island to island
with her daughter. 'Who can take Maria?' A strange house
on the other side of the bay takes her. There they have the means.
But that didn't make them good. The mask of piety cracks.
Maria's childhood ends too early, she's an unpaid servant
in perpetual coldness. Year after year. Perpetual seasickness
under the long oars, solemn terror
at table, the looks, the pike-skin scrunching
in her mouth: be grateful, be grateful.

                                        She never looked back
but because of that she could see what was new
and catch hold of it.
Out of encirclement.

I remember her. I would press close to her
and at the moment of death (the moment of crossing?) she sent out a
          thought
so that I – a five year old – understood what happened
half an hour before they rang.

Her I remember. But on the next brown photo
the unknown man –
dated by his clothes to the middle of last century.
A man around thirty: the vigorous eyebrows,
the face looking straight into my eyes
and whispering: 'here I am'.
But who 'I' am
there's no one any more who remembers. No one.

TB? Isolation?

Once coming up from the sea
on the stony slope steaming with grass he stopped
and felt the black bandage on his eyes.

Here, behind dense thickets – is it the island's oldest house?
The low, two-centuries-old fisherman's hut, log-cabin style, with
          heavy coarse grey timbers.
And the modern brass padlock has clicked it all together and shines
          like the ring in the nose of an old bull
who refuses to get up.
So much wood crouching. On the roof the ancient tiles which have
          slipped downways and crossways over each other
(the original pattern deranged over the years by the rotation of the
          earth)
it reminds me of something . . . I was there . . . wait: it's the old Jewish
          cemetery in Prague
where the dead live more packed than they were in life, the stones
          packed packed.
So much love encircled! The tiles with their lichen-script in an unknown
          tongue
are the stones in the ghetto cemetery of the archipelago folk, the stones
          raised and tumbled. –
The hovel is lit up
with all those who were driven by a certain wave, by a certain wind
right out here to their fates.

THE TRUTH-BARRIER
SANNINGSBARRIÄREN
(1978)

Citoyens

The night after the accident I dreamt of a pock-marked man
who walked through the alleys singing.
Danton!
Not the other one – Robespierre doesn't take such walks,
Robespierre spends a careful hour each morning on his toilette,
the rest of the day he devotes to The People.
In the paradise of the pamphlets, among the machines of virtue.
Danton –
or the man who wore his mask –
seemed to be standing on stilts.
I saw his face from beneath.
Like the scarred moon,
half in light, half in mourning.
I wanted to say something.
A weight in the breast, the plummet
that makes the clocks go,
the hands turn: year 1, year 2 . . .
A sharp scent like sawdust in the tiger-stalls.
And – as always in dreams – no sun.
But the walls were shining
in the alleys that curved
down to the waiting-room, the curved room,
the waiting-room where we all . . .

The Crossing-Place

Ice-wind in my eyes and the suns dance
in the kaleidoscope of tears as I cross
the street that's followed me so long, the street
where Greenland-summer shines from puddles.

Around me the whole strength of the street swarms,
power that remembers nothing, wants nothing.
For a thousand years, in the earth deep
under traffic the unborn forest quietly waits.

I get the idea that the street can see me.
Its sight is so dim the sun itself
is a grey ball in a black space.
But right now I am shining! The street sees me.

The Clearing

Deep in the forest there's an unexpected clearing which can be reached only by someone who has lost his way.

The clearing is enclosed in a forest that is choking itself. Black trunks with the ashy beard-stubble of lichen. The trees are screwed tightly together and are dead right up to the tops, where a few solitary green twigs touch the light. Beneath them: shadow brooding on shadow, and the swamp growing.

But in the open space the grass is strangely green and living. There are big stones lying here as if they'd been arranged. They must be the foundation stones of a house, but I could be wrong. Who lived here? No one can tell us. The names exist somewhere in an archive that no one opens (it's only archives that stay young). The oral tradition has died and with it the memories. The gypsy people remember but those who have learnt to write forget. Write down, and forget.

The homestead murmurs with voices, it is the centre of the world. But the inhabitants die or move out, the chronicle breaks off. Desolate for many years. And the homestead becomes a sphinx. At last everything's gone, except the foundation stones.

Somehow I've been here before, but now I must go. I dive in among the thickets. I can push my way through only with one step forward and two to the side, like a chess knight. Bit by bit the forest thins and lightens. My steps get longer. A footpath creeps towards me. I am back in the communications network.

On the humming electricity-post a beetle is sitting in the sun. Beneath the shining wing-covers its wings are folded up as ingeniously as a parachute packed by an expert.

How the Late Autumn Night Novel Begins

The ferry-boat smells of oil and something rattles all the time like an obsession. The spotlight's turned on. We're pulling in to the jetty. I'm the only one who wants off here. 'Need the gangway?' No. I take a long tottering stride right into the night and stand on the jetty, on the island. I feel wet and unwieldy, a butterfly just crept out of its cocoon, the plastic bags in each hand hang like misshapen wings. I turn round and see the boat gliding away with its shining windows, then grope my way towards the house which has been empty for so long. There's no one in any of the houses round about . . . It's good to fall asleep here. I lie on my back and don't know if I'm asleep or awake. Some books I've read pass by like old sailing ships on their way to the Bermuda triangle to vanish without trace . . . I hear a hollow sound, an absent-minded drumming. An object the wind keeps knocking against something the earth holds still. If the night is not just an absence of light, if the night really *is* something, then it's that sound. Stethoscope noises from a slow heart, it beats, goes silent for a time, comes back. As if the creature were moving in a zigzag across the Frontier. Or someone knocking in a wall, someone who belongs to the other world but was left behind here, knocking, wanting back. Too late. Couldn't get down there, couldn't get up there, couldn't get aboard . . . The other world is this world too. Next morning I see a sizzling golden-brown branch. A crawling stack of roots. Stones with faces. The forest is full of abandoned monsters which I love.

To Mats and Laila

The Dateline stays still between Samoa and Tonga but the Midnight-line glides forward over the ocean and the islands and the roofs of cabins. They're sleeping there, on the other side. Here in Värmland it's broad daylight, a day in early summer with a burning sun – I've thrown aside my luggage. A swim in the sky, the air's so blue . . . Then suddenly I see the ridges on the other side of the lake: they are clean-cut. Like the shaved parts of a patient's crown before he has a brain operation. It's been there all the time, I haven't seen it until now. Blinkers and a stiff neck . . . The journey continues. The landscape is now full of hatching and lines, like the old engravings where people moved about

small between hills and mountains which resembled anthills and villages
which were also thousands of strokes. And each man-ant brought his
own little stroke to add to the big engraving, there was no proper centre
but everything was alive. Something else: the figures are small but each
has his own face, the engraver has not denied them that – they are no
ants. Most of them are simple people but they can write their names.
Proteus on the other hand is a modern man who expresses himself
fluently in every style, comes with a "straight message" or empty
flourishes depending on which gang he belongs to at that moment. He
can't write his name. He shies away from it like the werewolf from the
silver bullet. They don't ask for it either, the hydra of the Company or
the hydra of the State . . . The journey continues. In this house there
lives a man who became desperate one evening and shot at the empty
hammock swaying above the grass. And the Midnight-line comes closer,
it'll soon have covered half its course. (And don't make out I want to
turn the clock back.) Tiredness will stream in through the hole left by
the sun . . . For me it's never happened that the diamond of a certain
moment cut an indelible score across the world-picture. No, it was wear
and tear that rubbed out the bright strange smile. But something's in
the process of becoming visible again, it's being worn *in*, begins to look
like a smile, no one knows what it's worth. Unaccounted for. There's
someone catches at my arm each time I try to write.

From the Winter of 1947

Days at school, that muffled thronging fortress.
At dusk I walked home under the shop-signs.
Then the whispering without lips: 'Wake up, sleepwalker!'
And every object pointed to The Room.

Fifth floor, a view of the yard. The lamp burned
in a circle of terror night after night.
I sat in bed without eyelids, saw filmstrips
filmstrips with the thoughts of insane people.

As if it were necessary . . .
As if the last childhood were being broken up
to make it pass through the grid.
As if it were necessary . . .

I read in books of glass but saw only the other:
the stains pushing through the wallpaper.
It was the living dead
who wanted their portraits painted . . .

Till dawn when the dustmen came
clattering the metal bins down there.
The back yard's peaceful grey bells
ringing me to sleep.

Schubertiana

1

In the evening darkness in a place outside New York, an outlook point
        where one single glance will encompass the homes of eight
        million people.
The giant city over there is a long shimmering drift, a spiral galaxy
        seen from the side.
Within the galaxy coffee-cups are pushed across the counter, the
        shop-windows beg from passers-by, a flurry of shoes that leave
        no prints.
The climbing fire escapes, the lift doors that glide shut, behind doors
        with police locks a perpetual seethe of voices.
Slouched bodies doze in subway coaches, the hurtling catacombs.
I know too – without statistics – that right now Schubert is being played
        in some room over there and that for someone the notes are
        more real than all the rest.

2

The endless expanses of the human brain are crumpled to the size
        of a fist.
In April the swallow returns to last year's nest under the guttering of
        this very barn in this very parish.
She flies from Transvaal, passes the equator, flies for six weeks over
        two continents, makes for precisely this vanishing dot in the
        land-mass.
And the man who catches the signals from a whole life in a few ordinary
        chords for five strings,

who makes a river flow through the eye of a needle,
is a stout young gentleman from Vienna known to his friends as 'The
          Mushroom', who slept with his glasses on
and stood at his writing desk punctually of a morning.
And then the wonderful centipedes of his manuscript were set in
motion.

3

The string quintet is playing. I walk home through warm forests with
          the ground springy under me,
curl up like an embryo, fall asleep, roll weightless into the future,
          suddenly feel that the plants have thoughts.

4

So much we have to trust, simply to live through our daily day without
          sinking through the earth!
Trust the piled snow clinging to the mountain slope above the village.
Trust the promises of silence and the smile of understanding, trust
          that the accident telegram isn't for us and that the sudden
          axe-blow from within won't come.
Trust the axles that carry us on the highway in the middle of the three
          hundred times life-size bee-swarm of steel.
But none of that is really worth our confidence.
The five strings say we can trust something else. And they keep us
          company part of the way there.
As when the time-switch clicks off in the stairwell and the fingers –
          trustingly – follow the blind handrail that finds its way in the
          darkness.

5

We squeeze together at the piano and play with four hands in F minor,
          two coachmen on the same coach, it looks a little ridiculous.
The hands seem to be moving resonant weights to and fro, as if we
          were tampering with the counterweights
in an effort to disturb the great scale arm's terrible balance: joy and
          suffering weighing exactly the same.
Annie said, 'This music is so heroic,' and she's right.
But those whose eyes enviously follow men of action, who secretly
          despise themselves for not being murderers,
don't recognise themselves here,

and the many who buy and sell people and believe that everyone can
        be bought, don't recognise themselves here.
Not their music. The long melody that remains itself in all its
        transformations, sometimes glittering and pliant, sometimes
        rugged and strong, snail-track and steel wire.
The perpetual humming that follows us – now –
up
the depths.

The Gallery

I stayed overnight at a motel by the E3.
In my room a smell I'd felt before
in the oriental halls of a museum:

masks Tibetan Japanese on a pale wall.

But it's not masks now, it's faces

forcing through the white wall of oblivion
to breathe, to ask about something.
I lie awake watching them struggle
and disappear and return.

Some lend each other features, exchange faces
far inside me
where oblivion and memory wheel-and-deal.

They force through oblivion's second coat
the white wall
they fade-out fade-in.

Here is a sorrow that doesn't call itself sorrow.

Welcome to the authentic galleries!
Welcome to the authentic galleys!
The authentic grilles!

The karate boy who paralysed someone
is still dreaming of fast money.

This woman keeps buying things
to toss in the hungry mouth of the vacuum
sneaking up behind her.

Mr X doesn't dare go out.
A dark stockade of ambiguous people
stands between him
and the steadily retreating horizon.

She who once fled from Karelia
she who could laugh . . .
now shows herself
but dumb, petrified, a statue from Sumer.

As when I was ten and came home late.
In the stairwell the light switched off
but the lift I stood in was bright, it rose
like a diving-bell through black depths
floor by floor while imagined faces
pressed against the grille . . .

But the faces are not imagined now, they are real.

I lie straight out like a cross-street.

Many step out from the white mist.
We touched each other once – we did!

A long bright carbolic-scented corridor.
The wheelchair. The teenage girl
learning to talk after the car-crash.

He who tried to call out under water
and the world's cold mass poured in
through nose and mouth.

Voices in the microphone said: Speed is power
speed is power!
Play the game, the show must go on!

We move through our career stiffly, step by step,
it's like a Noh play
with masks, high-pitched song: It's me, it's me!
The one who's failed
is represented by a rolled-up blanket.

An artist said: Before, I was a planet
with its own dense atmosphere.
Entering rays were broken into rainbows.
Perpetual raging thunderstorms, within.

Now I'm extinct and dry and open.
I no longer have childlike energy.
I have a hot side and a cold side.

No rainbows.

I stayed overnight in the echoing house.
Many want to come in through the walls
but most of them can't make it:

they're overcome by the white hiss of oblivion.

Anonymous singing drowns in the walls.
Discreet tappings that don't want to be heard
drawn-out sighs
my old repartees creeping homelessly.

Listen to society's mechanical self-reproaches
the voice of the big fan
like the artificial wind in mine tunnels
six hundred metres down.

Our eyes keep wide open under the bandages.

If I could at least make them realise
that this trembling beneath us
means we are on a bridge.

Often I have to stand motionless.
I am the knife-thrower's partner at a circus!
Questions I tossed aside in rage
come whining back

don't hit me, but nail down my shape
my rough outline
and stay in place when I've walked away.

Often I have to be silent. Voluntarily!
Because 'the last word' is said again and again.
Because good-day and good-bye . . .
Because this very day . . .

Because the margins rise at last
over their brims
and flood the text.

I stayed overnight at the sleepwalker's motel.
Many faces here are desperate
others smoothed out
after the pilgrim's walk through oblivion.

They breathe vanish struggle back again
they look past me
they all want to reach the icon of justice.

It happens rarely
that one of us really *sees* the other:

a person shows himself for an instant
as in a photograph but clearer
and in the background
something which is bigger than his shadow.

He's standing full-length before a mountain.
It's more a snail's shell than a mountain.
It's more a house than a snail's shell.
It's not a house but has many rooms.
It's indistinct but overwhelming.
He grows out of it, it out of him.
It's his life, it's his labyrinth.

Below Zero

We are at a party that doesn't love us. At last the party lets its mask drop and shows itself for what it really is: a marshalling yard. Cold colossi stand on rails in the mist. A piece of chalk has scribbled on the wagon doors.

It shouldn't be said but there is much suppressed violence here. That's why the components are so heavy. And why it's so hard to see something else that's there too: a little reflection from a mirror, flitting on the house-walls and gliding through the unknowing forest of glimmering faces, a biblical text which was never written: 'Come unto me, for I am full of contradictions like you.'

Tomorrow I am working in another town. I swish towards it through the morning hour which is like a big dark-blue cylinder. Orion hangs above the ground-frost. Children are standing in a silent cluster waiting for the school bus, children no one prays for. The light is growing as slowly as our hair.

The Boat and the Village

A Portuguese fishing-boat, blue, the wash rolls up the Atlantic a little.
A blue speck far out, but still I'm there, the six aboard don't notice
        we're seven.

I saw such a boat being built, it lay like a big lute without strings
in Poor Valley, the village where they wash and wash in fury, patience,
        melancholy.

The shore black with people, some meeting breaking up, the
        loudspeakers being carried away.
Soldiers led the speaker's Mercedes through the crush, words
        drummed on its metal sides.

The Black Mountains

At the next bend the bus broke free of the mountain's cold shadow,
turned its nose to the sun and crept roaring upwards.
We were packed in. The dictator's bust was there too,
wrapped in newspaper. A bottle passed from mouth to mouth.
Death, the birthmark, was growing on all of us, quicker on some,
          slower on others.
Up in the mountains the blue sea caught up with the sky.

Homewards

A telephone call ran out in the night and glittered over the countryside
          and in the suburbs.
Afterwards I slept uneasily in the hotel bed.
I was like the needle in a compass carried through the forest by an
          orienteer with a thumping heart.

After a Long Drought

The summer's grey right now strange evening.
The rain steals down from the sky
and lands quietly as if
it had to overpower someone sleeping.

The water-rings jostle on the bay's surface
and that is the only surface there is –
the other is height and depth
soar and sink.

Two pine-stems
shoot up and end in long hollow signal-drums.
Gone are the cities and the sun.
The thunder's in the tall grass.

It's possible to ring up the mirage island.
It's possible to hear the grey voice.
Iron-ore is honey for the thunder.
It's possible to live with one's code.

A Place in the Forest

On the way there a pair of startled wings clattered up, that was all. You
go there alone. There is a tall building which consists entirely of cracks,
a building which is perpetually tottering but can never collapse. The
thousand-fold sun floats in through the cracks. In this play of light an
inverted law of gravity prevails: the house is anchored in the sky and
whatever falls, falls upwards. You can turn round there. There you are
allowed to grieve. You can dare to see certain old truths which are
otherwise kept packed, in storage. The roles I have, deep down, float
up there, hang like the dried skulls in the ancestral cabin on some
out-of-the-way Melanesian islet. A childlike aura round the gruesome
trophies. So mild it is, in the forest.

Funchal

The fish-restaurant on the beach, simple, a shack built by ship-wrecked
people. Many turn away at the door, but not the gusts from the sea. A
shadow stands in his reeking cabin frying two fish according to an old
recipe from Atlantis, small explosions of garlic, oil running over the
tomato slices. Every bite says that the ocean wishes us well, a humming
from the deeps.

She and I look into each other. Like climbing up the wild blossoming hillsides without feeling the least tiredness. We're on the side of the animals, we're welcome, we don't get older. But over the years we've experienced so much together, we remember that, also times we were good for nothing (as when we queued up to give blood to the flourishing giant – he'd ordered transfusions), things that would've separated us if they hadn't brought us closer, and things we forgot together – but they have not forgotten us. They've become stones, dark ones and light ones. Stones in a scattered mosaic. And now it happens: the bits fly together, the mosaic is visible. It's waiting for us. It's shining from the wall in our hotel room, a design both violent and tender, perhaps a face, we haven't time to notice everything as we pull off our clothes . . .

At dusk we go out. The cape's enormous dark blue paw lies sprawled in the sea. We step into the human whirlpool, pushed around in a friendly way, soft controls, everyone chattering in that foreign language. 'No man is an island.' We become stronger through them, but also through ourselves. Through that within us which the other can't see. Which can meet only itself. The innermost paradox, the garage flower, the ventilator to the good darkness. A drink that bubbles in empty glasses. A loudspeaker that sends out silence. A pathway that grows over again behind each step. A book that can be read only in the dark.

THE WILD MARKET-SQUARE
DET VILDA TORGET
(1983)

Brief Pause in the Organ Recital

The organ stops playing and it's deathly quiet in the church, but only
        for a couple of seconds.
And the faint rumbling penetrates from the traffic out there, that
        greater organ.

For we are surrounded by the murmuring of the traffic, it flows along
        the cathedral walls.
The outer world glides there like a transparent film and with shadows
        struggling pianissimo.

And as if it were part of the street noise I hear one of my pulses beating
        in the silence,
I hear my blood circulating, the cascade that hides inside me, that
        I walk about with,

and as close as my blood and as far away as a memory from when
        I was four
I hear the trailer that rumbles past and makes the six-hundred-year-old
        walls tremble.

This could hardly be less like a mother's lap, yet at the moment I am
        a child,
hearing the grown-ups talking far away, the voices of the winners and
        the losers mingling.

On the blue benches a sparse congregation. And the pillars rise like
        strange trees:
no roots (only the common floor) and no crown (only the common
        roof).

I relive a dream. That I'm standing alone in a churchyard. Everywhere
        heather glows
as far as the eye can reach. Who am I waiting for? A friend. Why doesn't
        he come. He's here already.

Slowly death turns up the lights from underneath, from the ground.
        The heath shines, a stronger and stronger purple –
no, a colour no one has seen . . . until the morning's pale light whines
        in through the eyelids

and I waken to that unshakeable PERHAPS that carries me through
        the wavering world.
And each abstract picture of the world is as impossible as the
        blue-print of a storm.

At home stood the all-knowing Encyclopedia, a yard of bookshelf, in
        it I learnt to read.
But each one of us has his own encyclopedia written, it grows out of
        each soul,

it's written from birth onwards, the hundreds of thousands of pages
        stand pressed against each other
and yet with air between them! Like the quivering leaves in a forest.
        The book of contradictions.

What's there changes by the hour, the pictures retouch themselves,
        the words flicker.
A wake washes through the whole text, it's followed by the next wave,
        and then the next . . .

From March 1979

Weary of all who come with words, words but no language
I make my way to the snow-covered island.
The untamed has no words.
The unwritten pages spread out on every side!
I come upon the tracks of deer's hooves in the snow.
Language but no words.

The Memories Watch Me

A June morning, too soon to wake,
too late to fall asleep again.

I must go out – the greenery is dense
with memories, they follow me with their gaze.

They can't be seen, they merge completely with
the background, true chameleons.

They are so close that I can hear them breathe
although the birdsong here is deafening.

Winter's Gaze

I lean like a ladder and with my face
reach in to the second floor of the cherry tree.
I'm inside the bell of colours, it chimes with sunlight.
I polish off the swarthy red berries faster than four magpies.

A sudden chill, from a great distance, meets me.
The moment blackens
and remains like an axe-cut in a tree-trunk.

From now on it's late. We make off half-running
out of sight, down, down in the ancient sewage system.
The tunnels. We walk about there for months
half in service and half in flight.

Brief devotions when some hatchway opens above us
and a weak light falls.
We look up: the starry sky through the grating.

The Station

A train has just rolled in. Coach after coach stand here,
but no doors open, no one gets off or on.
Are there no doors at all? Inside, a crowd
of shut-in figures stirring to and fro.
Gazing out through immovable window-panes.
Outside, a man who walks along the coaches with a hammer.
He strikes the wheels, a feeble clang. Except for here!
Here the chime swells unbelievably: a lightning stroke,
peal of cathedral bells, a sailing-round-the-world peal
that lifts the whole train and the landscape's wet stones.
Everything is singing. This you will remember. Travel on!

Answers to Letters

In the bottom drawer of my desk I come across a letter that first arrived twenty-six years ago. A letter in panic, and it's still breathing when it arrives the second time.

A house has five windows: through four of them the day shines clear and still. The fifth faces a black sky, thunder and storm. I stand at the fifth window. The letter.

Sometimes an abyss opens between Tuesday and Wednesday but twenty-six years may be passed in a moment. Time is not a straight line, it's more of a labyrinth, and if you press close to the wall at the right place you can hear the hurrying steps and the voices, you can hear yourself walking past there on the other side.

Was the letter ever answered? I don't remember, it *was* long ago. The countless thresholds of the sea went on migrating. The heart went on leaping from second to second like the toad in the wet grass of an August night.

The unanswered letters pile up, like cirro-stratus clouds promising bad weather. They make the sunbeams lustreless. One day I will answer. One day when I am dead and can at last concentrate. Or at least so far away from here that I can find myself again. When I'm walking, newly arrived, in the big city, on 125th Street, in the wind on the street of dancing garbage. I who love to stray off and vanish in the crowd, a capital T in the mass of the endless text.

Icelandic Hurricane

Not earth-tremor but sky-quake. Turner could have painted it, lashed tight. A solitary mitt has just whirled by, several miles from its hand. I am going to make my way against the wind to that house on the other side of the field. I flutter in the hurricane. I am X-rayed, the skeleton hands in its resignation. Panic grows as I cross, I founder, I founder and drown on dry land! How heavy, everything I suddenly have to drag along, how heavy for the butterfly to tow a barge! There at last. A final wrestle with the door. And now inside. And now inside. Behind the big glass pane. What a strange and wonderful invention glass is – to be close yet untouched . . . Outside, a horde of transparent sprinters in giant format charges across the lava plain. But I'm no longer fluttering. I'm sitting behind the glass, at rest, my own portrait.

The Blue Wind-Flowers

To be spell-bound – nothing's easier. It's one of the oldest tricks of the soil and springtime: the blue wind-flowers. They are in a way unexpected. They shoot up out of the brown rustle of last year in overlooked places where one's gaze never pauses. They glimmer and float, yes, float, and that comes from their colour. That sharp violet-blue now weighs nothing. Here is ecstasy, but low-voiced. "Career" – irrelevant! "Power" and "publicity" – ridiculous! They must have laid on a great reception up in Nineveh, with pompe and "Trompe up!". Raising the rafters. And above all those brows the crowning crystal chandeliers hung like glass vultures. Instead of such an over-decorated and strident cul-de-sac, the wind-flowers open a secret passage to the real celebration, which is quiet as death.

The Blue House

It is a night of radiant sun. I stand in the dense forest and look away towards my house with its haze-blue walls. As if I had just died and was seeing the house from a new angle.

It has stood for more than eighty summers. Its wood is impregnated with four times joy and three times sorrow. When someone who lived in the house dies, it is repainted. The dead person himself is painting, without a brush, from inside.

Beyond the house, open ground. Once a garden, now grown over. Stationary breakers of weed, pagodas of weed, welling text, upanishads of weed, a viking fleet of weed, dragon-heads, lances, a weed-empire!

Across the overgrown garden there flutters the shadow of a boomerang that is thrown again and again. It has something to do with a person who lived in the house long before my time. Almost a child. An impulse comes from him, a thought, a thought like an act of will: 'make . . . draw . . .' To reach out of his fate.

The house is like a child's drawing. A deputising childishness that grew because someone – much too soon – gave up his mission to be a child. Open the door, step in! In here there's unrest in the ceiling and peace in the walls. Above the bed hangs a painting of a ship with seventeen sails, hissing wave-crests and a wind that the gilt frame can't contain.

It's always so early in here, before the crossroads, before the irrevocable choices. Thank you for this life! Still I miss the alternatives. The sketches, all of them, want to become real.

A motor far away on the water expands the summer-night horizon. Both joy and sorrow swell in the dew's magnifying glass. Without really knowing, we divine; our life has a sister ship, following quite another route. While the sun blazes behind the islands.

Satellite Eyes

The ground is rough, no mirror.
Only the coarsest of spirits
can reflect themselves there: the Moon
and the Ice Age.

Come closer in the dragon-haze!
Heavy clouds, milling streets.
A rustling downpour of souls.
Barrack-squares.

Nineteen Hundred and Eighty

His glance flits in jerks across the newsprint.
Feelings come, so icy they're taken for thoughts.
Only in deep hypnosis could he be his other I,
his hidden sister, the woman who joins the hundreds of thousands
screaming 'Death to the Shah!' – although he is already dead –
a marching black tent, pious and full of hate.
Jihad! Two who shall never meet take the world in hand.

Black Picture-Postcards

I

The diary written full, future unknown.
The cable hums the folk-song with no home.
Snow-fall on the lead-still sea. Shadows
                    wrestle on the pier.

II

In the middle of life it happens that death comes
and takes man's measurements. The visit
is forgotten and life goes on. But the suit
                        is sewn on the quiet.

Fire-Jottings

Throughout the dismal months my life sparkled alive only when I made
        love with you.
As the firefly ignites and fades out, ignites and fades out, – in glimpses
        we can trace its flight
in the dark among the olive trees.

Throughout the dismal months the soul lay shrunken, lifeless,
but the body went straight to you.
The night sky bellowed.
Stealthily we milked the cosmos and survived.

Many Steps

The icons are laid in the earth face up
and the earth trod down again
by wheels and shoes, by thousands of steps,
by the heavy steps of ten thousand doubters.

In my dream I stepped down into a luminous underground pool,
a surging litany.
What sharp longing! What idiotic hope!
And over me the tread of millions of doubters.

Postludium

I drag like a grapnel over the world's floor –
everything catches that I don't need.
Tired indignation. Glowing resignation.
The executioners fetch stone. God writes in the sand.

Silent rooms.
The furniture stands in the moonlight, ready to fly.
I walk slowly into myself
through a forest of empty suits of armour.

Dream Seminar

Four thousand million on earth.
They all sleep, they all dream.
Faces throng, and bodies, in each dream –
the dreamt-of people are more numerous
than us. But take no space . . .
You doze off at the theatre perhaps,
in mid-play your eyelids sink.
A fleeting double-exposure: the stage
before you out-manoeuvred by a dream.
Then no more stage, it's you.
The theatre in the honest depths!
The mystery of the overworked director!
Perpetual memorising of new plays . . .
A bedroom. Night.
The darkened sky is flowing through the room.
The book that someone fell asleep from lies
still open
sprawling wounded at the edge of the bed.
The sleeper's eyes are moving,
they're following the text without letters
in another book –
illuminated, old-fashioned, swift.
A dizzying commedia inscribed
within the eyelids' monastery walls.

A unique copy. Here, this very moment.
In the morning, wiped out.
The mystery of the great waste!
Annihilation. As when suspicious men
in uniforms stop the tourist –
open his camera, unwind the film
and let the daylight kill the pictures:
thus dreams are blackened by the light of day.
Annihilated or just invisible?
There is a kind of out-of-sight dreaming
that never stops. Light for other eyes.
A zone where creeping thoughts learn to walk.
Faces and forms regrouped.
We're moving on a street, among people
in blazing sun.
But just as many – maybe more –
we don't see
are also there in dark buildings
high on both sides.
Sometimes one of them comes to the window
and glances down on us.

Codex

Men of footnotes, not headlines. I find myself in the deep corridor
that would have been dark
if my right hand wasn't shining like a torch.
The light falls on something written on the wall
and I see it
as the diver sees the name on the sunken hull flimmering towards him
        in the flowing depths:
ADAM ILEBORGH 1448. Who?
It was he who made the organ spread its clumpy wings and rise –
and it held itself airborne nearly a minute.
An experiment blessed with success!
Written on the wall: MAYONE, DAUTHENDEY, KAMINSKY . . . The light
        touches name upon name.
The walls are quite scrawled over.

They're the names of the all-but extinct artists
the men of footnotes, the unplayed, the half-forgotten, the immortal
        unknown.
For a moment it feels as if they're all whispering their names at once –
whispering added to whispering till a tumbling breaker cascades along
        the corridor
without throwing anyone down.
Though the corridor is no longer a corridor.
Neither a graveyard nor a market-place but something of both.
A kind of green-house too.
Plenty of oxygen here.
Dead men of the footnotes can breathe deeply, they remain in the
        ecological system.
But there is much they are spared.
They are spared swallowing the morality of power,
they are spared the black-and-white chequered game where the smell
        of corpses is the only thing that never dies.
They are rehabilitated.
And those who can no longer receive
have not stopped giving.
They rolled out a little of the radiant and melancholy tapestry
and let go again.
Some are anonymous, they are my friends
without my knowing them, they are like those stone-people
carved on grave-slabs in old churches.
Soft or harsh reliefs in walls we brush against, figures and names
sunk in the stone floors, on the way to extinction.
But those who really want to be struck from the list . . .
They don't stop in the region of footnotes,
they step into the downward career that ends in oblivion and peace.
Total oblivion. It's a kind of exam
taken in silence: to step over the border without anyone noticing . . .

Carillon

Madame despises her guests because they want to stay at her shabby
    hotel.
I have the corner-room, one floor up: a wretched bed, a lightbulb in
    the ceiling.
Heavy drapes where a quarter of a million mites are on the march.

Outside, a pedestrian street
with slow tourists, hurrying school-children, men in working-clothes
    who wheel their rattling bikes.
Those who think they make the earth go round and those who think
    they go round helplessly in earth's grip.
A street we all walk, where does it emerge?

The room's only window faces something else: The Wild Market
    Square,
ground that seethes, a wide trembling surface, at times crowded and
    at times deserted.

What I carry within me is materialised there, all terrors, all expectations.
All the inconceivable that will nevertheless happen.

I have low beaches, if death rises six inches I shall be flooded.
I am Maximilian. It's 1488. I'm held prisoner here in Bruges
because my enemies are irresolute –
they are wicked idealists and what they did in horror's back-yard I can't
    describe, I can't turn blood into ink.

I am also the man in overalls wheeling his rattling bike down on the
    street.

I am also the person seen, that tourist, the one loitering and pausing,
    loitering and pausing
and letting his gaze wander over the pale moon-tanned faces and surging
    draperies of the old paintings.

No one decides where I go, least of all myself, though each step is where
    it must be.
Walking round in the fossil-wars where all are invulnerable because
    all are dead!

The dusty foliage, the walls with their loop-holes, the garden paths
    where petrified tears crunch under the heels . . .

Unexpectedly, as if I'd stepped on a trip-wire, the bell-ringing starts
    in the anonymous tower.
Carillon! The sack splits along its seams and the chimes roll out across
    Flanders.
Carillon! The cooing iron of the bells, hymn and hit-song in one, and
    tremblingly written in the air.
The shaky-handed doctor wrote out a prescription that no one can
    decipher but his writing will be recognised . . .

Over meadow and house-top, harvest and mart,
over quick and dead the carillon rings.
Christ and Antichrist, hard to tell apart!
The bells bear us home at last on their wings.

They have stopped.

I am back in the hotel room: the bed, the light, the drapes. There are
    strange noises, the cellar is dragging itself up the stairs.

I lie on the bed with my arms outstretched.
I am an anchor that has dug itself down and holds steady
the huge shadow floating up there,
the great unknown which I am a part of and which is certainly more
    important than me.

Outside, the walkway, the street where my steps die away and also what
    is written, my preface to silence and my inside-out psalm.

Molokai

We stand at the edge and deep down under us glisten the roofs of the
    leper colony.
The climb down we could manage but we'd never make it back up the
    slopes before nightfall.
So we turn back through the forest, walk among trees with long blue
    needles.

It's silent here, like the silence when the hawk is coming.

These are woods that forgive everything but forget nothing.

Damien, for love, chose life and obscurity. He received death and
      fame.

But we see these events from the wrong side: a heap of stones instead
      of the sphinx's face.

RECENT POEMS

The Forgotten Captain

We have many shadows. I was walking home
in the September night when Y
climbed out of his grave after forty years
and kept me company.

At first he was quite empty, only a name
but his thoughts swam
faster than time ran
and caught up with us.

I put his eyes to my eyes
and saw war's ocean.
The last boat he captained
took shape beneath us.

Ahead and astern the Atlantic convoy crept,
the ships that would survive
and the ships that bore the Mark
(invisible to all)

while sleepless days relieved each other
but never him.
Under his oilskin, his life-jacket.
He never came home.

It was an internal weeping that bled him to death
in a Cardiff hospital,
he could at last lie down
and turn into a horizon.

Goodbye, eleven-knot convoys! Goodbye, 1940!
Here ends world history.
The bombers were left hanging.
The heathery moors blossomed.

A photo from early this century shows a beach.
Six Sunday-best boys.
Sailing-boats in their arms.
What solemn airs!

The boats that became life and death for some of them.
And writing about the dead –
that too is a game made heavy
with what is to come.

The Nightingale in Badelunda

In the green midnight at the nightingale's northern limit. Heavy leaves
hang in trance, the deaf cars race towards the neon-line. The nightingale's
voice rises without wavering to the side, it is as penetrating as a cock-
crow, but beautiful and free of vanity. I was in prison and it visited me.
I was sick and it visited me. I didn't notice it then, but I do now. Time
streams down from the sun and the moon and into all the tick-tock-
thankful clocks. But right here there is no time. Only the nightingale's
voice, the raw resonant notes that whet the night sky's gleaming scythe.

Vermeer

No protected world . . . Just behind the wall the noise begins,
the inn is there
with laughter and bickering, rows of teeth, tears, the din of bells
and the deranged brother-in-law, the death-bringer we all must
            tremble for.

The big explosion and the tramp of rescue arriving late
the boats preening themselves on the straits, the money creeping down
            in the wrong man's pocket
demands stacked on demands
gaping red flowerheads sweating premonitions of war.

In from there and right through the wall into the clear studio
into the second that's allowed to live for centuries.
Pictures that call themselves 'The Music Lesson'
or 'Woman in Blue Reading a Letter' –
she's in her eighth month, two hearts kicking inside her.
On the wall behind is a crumpled map of Terra Incognita.

Breathe calmly . . . An unknown blue material nailed to the chairs.
The gold studs flew in with incredible speed
and stopped abruptly
as if they had never been other than stillness.

Ears sing, from depth or height.
It's the pressure from the other side of the wall
it makes each fact float
and steadies the brush.

It hurts to go through walls, it makes you ill
but it is necessary.
The world is one. But walls . . .
And the wall is part of yourself –
we know or we don't know, but it's true for us all
except for small children. No walls for them.

The clear sky has leant itself against the wall.
It's like a prayer to the emptiness.
And the emptiness turns its face to us
and whispers
'I am not empty, I am open.'

Index of titles and first lines

154

WRITERS PUBLISHED BY

BLOODAXE BOOKS

FLEUR ADCOCK	PAUL HYLAND
BASIL BUNTING	KATHLEEN JAMIE
ANGELA CARTER	B.S. JOHNSON
JOHN CASSIDY	JENNY JOSEPH
EILÉAN NÍ CHUILLEANÁIN	BRENDAN KENNELLY
STEWART CONN	DENISE LEVERTOV
DAVID CONSTANTINE	EDNA LONGLEY
JENI COUZYN	SHENA MACKAY
HART CRANE	SEAN O'BRIEN
ADAM CZERNIAWSKI	JOHN OLDHAM
PETER DIDSBURY	TOM PAULIN
JOHN DREW	IRINA RATUSHINSKAYA
HELEN DUNMORE	CAROL RUMENS
DOUGLAS DUNN	DAVID SCOTT
STEPHEN DUNSTAN	JAMES SIMMONS
G.F. DUTTON	MATT SIMPSON
LAURIS EDMOND	KEN SMITH
STEVE ELLIS	EDITH SÖDERGRAN
RUTH FAINLIGHT	MARIN SORESCU
EVA FIGES	LEOPOLD STAFF
TONY FLYNN	MARTIN STOKES
PAMELA GILLILAN	R.S. THOMAS
ANDREW GREIG	TOMAS TRANSTRÖMER
TONY HARRISON	MARINA TSVETAYEVA
MIROSLAV HOLUB	ALAN WEARNE
FRANCES HOROVITZ	NIGEL WELLS
DOUGLAS HOUSTON	JOHN HARTLEY WILLIAMS

*For a complete list of poetry, fiction, drama and photography books
published by Bloodaxe, please write to:*
**Bloodaxe Books Ltd, P.O. Box 1SN,
Newcastle upon Tyne NE99 1SN.**